MEMORY LANE
BURTON
AND SOUTH DERBYSHIRE

Burton Mail

MEMORY LANE
BURTON
AND SOUTH DERBYSHIRE

COMPILED BY
DAVE STACEY

First published in Great Britain byThe Breedon Books Publishing Company Limited
Breedon House, 44 Friar Gate, Derby, DE1 1DA. 1999

This paperback edition published in Great Britain in 2015 by DB Publishing, an imprint of
JMD Media Ltd

ISBN 978-1-78091-523-4

Printed and bound in the UK by Copytech (UK) Ltd Peterborough

Contents

Acknowledgements

WITHOUT the Herculean efforts of Andy Parker and Tracey Smith, this book would not have been possible. I also wish to thank Valerie Burton of Burton Civic Society, Ted Smith for pictures of soccer and the Staffordshire Yeomanry and for access to the wonderful collection of pictures and information amassed by his friend, the late Len Foster; Graham Nutt, Rob Cox and Ron Geary, Joe Fearn, Pauline and Norman Willey, Graham Parker, Cliff Collier, Derek Tedder, Timber Wood, Norman Binns, David Stanier, Rex Page, Kevin Kent, Ivor Gibbs, Walter Bullock, Captain Douglas Forrest and George Lawson. Apologies to anyone else I should have mentioned.

David Stacey
August 1999

Introduction

IN the last few years Burton and South Derbyshire has changed almost beyond recognition.

There is hardly a street or road that has not been altered in some way or other.

Long gone are the days when Burton was bedevilled by trains crossing and re-crossing its roads, and the coal mines with which many outsiders still associate South Derbyshire are also now just part of the past.

In fact the only memories of the way it used to be are those stored away in the minds of residents and in photographs from days gone by.

We know that readers of the *Burton Mail* are fascinated by our weekly feature, "The Mail Remembers", so painstakingly compiled by Dave Stacey, himself a familiar figure in the town.

So when it was suggested the *Mail* should use its library of photographs as the basis for this book, Dave was the obvious choice to put it together.

We set out to capture something of the way things used to be, capturing the images of the people of Burton and South Derbyshire at work, rest, play, and even war.

We hope that you enjoy perusing this book as much as we have enjoyed putting it together, and that for older readers it brings back happy memories and emotions, and for those whose memories do not go back that far, it provides an interesting spotlight on years gone by.

I am grateful to Dave for all his hard work in producing this book, together with colleagues at the *Mail* who helped him and the many other people who so kindly lent pictures for the book or passed on vital valuable information. Thank you.

Brian Vertigen
Editor
Burton Mail

Landmarks

One of a series of local views taken from an aircraft in late autumn 1966 by long-serving *Mail* photographer Maurice Woodcock. It shows the Winshill countryside beyond the then new Dalebrook housing estate. In the foreground is the River Trent which flows over a weir at the back of Greensmith's flour mill. Newton Road, linking Burton with Newton Solney and

Repton, can be seen and in the background, up Mill Hill Lane, is the Boys' Grammar School, later part of the Abbot Beyne Endowed (C) School.

Right: A landmark for many miles, the sight of which warms the hearts of returning travellers, is Winshill Water Tower, built in 1904 to make it easier for piped water to reach parts they otherwise reached only sometimes.

Far right: The Goat Maltings in Clarence Street, Burton, built by Peter Walker next to Anglesey Road brewery. He came from Wrexham, and

chose a Welsh mountain goat as the symbol of his firm. Though this is one of the town's best-loved landmarks, it has been allowed to fall into disrepair.

Bretby Orthopaedic Hospital, now closed, was in the former home of the Chesterfield family. Generations of people benefited from treatment there.

When the Earls and Countesses of Chesterfield lived at Bretby Hall it was believed that whenever a branch fell from the cedar tree in the grounds a member of the family would die. As the tree aged, the branches were held in place by chains. For most of the 20th century the hall was an orthopaedic hospital, now closed. The tree has been felled for safety reasons and others, not yet as impressive, have been planted.

When oldtimers in Burton and South Derbyshire play the double four at dominoes, they often say "Hartshorne Church". This is because the double four reminds them of the shape of St Peter's.

A rural scene in Main Street, Sudbury.

A peaceful South Derbyshire scene as the Twyford Ferry crosses the Trent.

The Stapenhill Gardens provide a colourful floral display for much of each year. With the adjoining Stapenhill Recreation Grounds they provide a pleasant spot for quiet leisure moments.

Kevin Kent, who took this unusual picture, calls it Holy Mass and Holy Bass. Just what is the flag of Bass, the brewers, doing on top of Burton parish church of St Modwen?

It was a trick shot. The flag was really on top of the brewery water tower, off High Street, as this picture from a slightly different angle reveals. Both were taken from windows of the telephone exchange in Fleet Street where Kevin used to work.

Awaiting demolition: the blacksmith's shop off Lichfield Street, Burton, still in use until shortly before redevelopment of the area in the 1980s.

Large areas in the centre of Burton, unchanged for generations, were transformed from the 1960s onwards. This picture by Kevin Kent in the late 1980s shows, exposed by the clearance for the Octagon shopping centre, a view of part of Burton General Hospital in New Street with its tall chimney. Hospital and chimney have since been replaced by housing.

For most of the years after the Second World War Burton's skyline has been dominated by the cooling towers of Drakelow Power Station, once the largest in Europe. Soon after Kevin Kent took this picture the four smaller ones, which can be seen on the right, were demolished, including the first one to go up in the 1950s.

The snow-covered statue of the Burton Cooper, the work of sculptor James Butler RA, in its original position facing Burton Market Place. In the 1990s, despite protests, it was moved inside the central area shopping centre, which was renamed Cooper's Square. The 100-year-old horse chestnut tree in the Market Place, on the right of the picture, was removed as unsafe in 1999, with the intention of planting a new tree to mark the Millennium. (Kevin Kent).

War and Remembrance

The 150ft-deep crater left by the 1944 accidental explosion of an underground ammunition dump at Fauld, near Hanbury, the biggest man-made explosion before the atom bomb dropped on Hiroshima. More than 3,500 tons of high explosive went up, 68 people died: 18 of them and a 300-acre farm were never seen again. A reservoir holding 6 million gallons gave way, and many of the deaths were because of this.

A village pub destroyed by the Fauld explosion.

A memorial at Hanbury to local people killed in action in the Second World War and in the 1944 Fauld explosion.

Burton men who joined the Staffordshire Yeomanry Territorial Army unit in Burton were mobilised on the outbreak of the Second World War. This picture shows them marching to the railway station within days of declaration of war. Among them is Ted Smith, who lent these pictures of the Yeomanry.

The Staffordshire Yeomanry on patrol in Palestine, near the Syrian border.

These Staffordshire Yeomanry trumpeters and buglers from Burton, pictured at Patshall Park Camp at Wolverhampton in 1939, were allocated to various squadrons of the regiment when war came. They are (left to right) Joe Samways, Ted Smith, Tom Harvey, Cyril Copeman and Nobby Potts and (front) Norman Robinson.

The Yeomanry were among the Desert Rats who fought at El Alemain and advanced to Tripoli. This picture shows Lt Col James Eadie, Officer Commanding the Staffordshire Yeomanry in the Western Desert, with Monty — General (later Field Marshal) Sir Bernard Law Montgomery — on the command tank Defiance. The Eadies were a Burton brewing family.

A Birmingham-made "swimming tank", one of those used by the Yeomanry to land in Normandy on D-Day and to cross the Elbe. They were also used at the Shelt Estuary in Holland.

One of the first post-war Staffordshire Yeomanry reunions at Burton.

The Burton area has a good record for supporting the Territorial Army and this picture was taken of a new recruit in 1973. In the past there have been TA units of the old North Staffordshire Regiment and the Staffordshire Yeomanry based in the town. Now there is a company of the Staffordshire Regiment.

Burton's War Memorial, erected after the First World War, where each year wreaths are laid to the memory of those killed in both world wars and other conflicts. Behind it stands Burton College, formerly known as the Technical College.

Remembrance Day at Swadlincote. A regular feature of the occasion is the laying of wreaths at the Memorial Gates of Eureka Park.

One of the oddities about Burton District Branch of the Burma Star Association is that its president for many years was not a veteran of the battles in the steaming jungles during the Second World War. Instead Stan Deeming served in the icy northern cold, escorting shipping convoys carrying urgent supplies from Britain to the Soviet Union. He took on the presidency to help out the branch. This picture shows the dedication of a seat provided by the branch in Stapenhill Gardens, where it has also provided a Burma Rose display. The branch's annual services have been held in nearby St Peter's Church.

Names That Made the News

Stretcher-bearer Lance Corporal W. H. (Bill) Coltman of the North Staffordshire Regiment, the only Burton man to be awarded the Victoria Cross, and probably the most decorated NCO in the British Army. During the First World War he won the Distinguished Conduct Medal and Bar and Military Medal and Bar before the VC, the latter for going out three times under fire to bring in wounded men including his own officer. A deeply religious man, he was proud that all his medals were for saving, not taking, lives. In Civvy Street he was a gardener for Burton Town Council's parks department. In the Territorial Army he held the rank of Captain and the present TA Headquarters in Wharf Road bears the name Coltman House.

Many local people remember when the father of film star John Hurt was vicar of Woodville. John has long been a top star, his films including *Elephant Man*, *Scandal* (in which he played Stephen Ward), *Contact* (in which he was an eccentric industrial billionaire) and *Alien*. The only other film stars the area can claim are Judy Gunn, who was in a Burton children's troupe called The Edgeleys before going on to movie fame, and Joan Rice, who lived with her grandmother in Blackpool Street, Burton, before becoming a glamour girl on the big screen.

Probably Burton's most famous son, Phil Seamen already showed his talent as a drummer while attending Stafford Street Infants' School. As a young man he played in a local band led by Len Reynolds, went full-time professional with nationally-known jazz trumpeter Nat Gonella, later working with Jack Parnell, Ronnie Scott, Harry South and with his friend and disciple, pop drummer Ginger Baker. When top American jazz drummer Buddy Rich was invited to play in Britain he said, "I don't know why you want me, when you have Phil Seamen." Another tribute came from blues giant Jimmy Witherspoon who called Phil "the world's greatest jazz drummer." Phil died in his mid-40s in 1972.

Burton-born Armsbee Bancroft learned to play the piano at eight, then took up the organ. At 11 he became assistant organist at Mosley Street Methodist Church, then for 27 years was organist and choirmaster for Victoria Street Methodists.

He played piano in local dance bands, then set up his own quartet which played regularly at the Stanhope Arms Hotel and other venues for 20 years.

Armsbee became famous nationally playing theatre organ dates, including Blackpool Tower organ, and broadcast on Radio Algiers, Radio France and the BBC. He accompanied Ken Dodd and other top artistes. He also played quite often in Holland.

Armsbee with Graham Parker, his drummer in the quartet at the Stanhope.

Mr John Jennings, Burton MP from 1955 to 1974, who had been headmaster of the village school at Netherseal, was always ready to listen to his constituents. This picture shows him receiving a petition on a local issue.

South Derbyshire's MP for several years, Mrs Edwina Currie, was a junior health minister until her warning about danger from eggs incensed producers. Eventually she switched from politics to writing novels.

To celebrate his first 20 years as Conservative MP for Burton, a party was thrown for Sir Ivan Lawrence QC at the home of millionaire property developer Mr Stan Clarke and and his wife, Hilda, at Barton-under-Needwood in 1994. Pictured are (left to right) Mr George Lawson, who organised the event, Mrs Eda Rose Lawson, the Rt Hon Lord Tebbit of Chingford, Lady Lawrence, Miss Rachel Lawrence, Sir Ivan Lawrence, Margaret the Lady Thatcher, Sir Dennis Thatcher, Mrs Hilda Clarke, Mr Stan Clarke, Mrs Amanda Boardman-Weston, Mr Simon Boardman-Weston, Mrs Gillian Priestnall, Sir Bernard Ingham and Mr Keith Hornby Priestnall. Sir Ivan was MP from 1974 to 1997.

The last Mayor of Burton County Borough was Councillor Harry Buckingham in 1973. Afterwards the area had two civic dignitaries, a town mayor and a chairman of East Staffordshire District, until in the 1990s it was decided to make East Staffordshire a borough with a mayor and not to have any more mayors of Burton.

World of Work

Burton celebrates the visit of King Edward VII who, in 1902, pulled a lever to start the brewing of Bass's King's Ale. More than half a century later precious unopened bottles of this strong brew sold for as much as £600, often for charity.

A forest of chimneys is shown in this view of Burton breweries looking north from Burton Parish Church of St Modwen. The brewery water tower remains, but much of what can be seen on this picture has gone completely.

The Burton Union system of brewing, unique to the town, in which the ale is allowed to ferment in huge casks. Only at Marston's is this system, which local brewers used to claim gave local beer its distinctive taste, continued, but some unions are on display in the grounds of the Bass Museum.

A trussing-in ceremony at which a trainee cooper, on completing his apprenticeship, was rolled in a barrel of his own making and covered in beer and wood shavings (sometimes worse) before joining his mates in a glorious drinking session. Sadly, not all were kept on as qualified coopers after this ordeal; it was cheaper to employ more youngsters.

Brewery buildings long stood between Burton town centre and the river like this one, built in 1880. In April, 1974, a few days after Ian Hickman of Newhall took this picture, now in the Civic Society collection, this one, by then no longer needed, burned down in a spectacular fire.

Allsopp's Lager Brewery, which in the early part of the century stood in High Street, Burton.

This picture of a mass of people at Bass's serves as a reminder that the breweries were once the main employers of labour in Burton. Avout half the working population had brewery jobs, about 3,500 working for Bass. Huge reductions in the brewing workforce came in the second half of the 20th century.

Peter Walker and Co's Brewery in Clarence Street (there was also a Peter Walker and Sons at Shobnall Road). Once the town had 31 breweries. Those that have disappeared through mergers, closures or moves out of town include Truman's, Everards, Salt's, Charrington's, Allsopp's, Robinson's, Bindley's, Worthington's, Evershed's, Burton Brewery Co and others. The biggest shocks came when Ind Coope Burton Brewery became Carlsberg-Tetley, and then was bought by Bass.

High Street level crossing, seen from the brewery.

The United Kingdom's first registered trade mark. A Bass employee camped all night outside the trade mark office to be certain of being first in on the opening day so that the firm could claim trade mark number one.

The last train at Horninglow Street level crossing on July 21, 1967. The network of railways serving the breweries criss-crossed the town centre roads, but their period of usefulness had come to an end.

There were coal mines throughout South Derbyshire but gradually the number was reduced until finally there were none left. Once miners from Scotland were encouraged to move into the area. The time came when local miners had to seek work in distant pits or in the Burton breweries.

Hall's Collieries in South Derbyshire sold direct to householders using the slogan "Hall's, the King of Coals."

A loco at Cadley Hill Colliery.

The Free Library at Alexandra Road, Swadlincote, paid for out of charitable funds provided by US philanthropist Andrew Carnegie, eventually became unusable because of mining subsidence. Trolleys laden with books would roll along the floor which developed a pronounced slope because of the ravages of subsidence. Eventually a more modern library was built in Civic Way.

Another victim of mining subsidence was Swadlincote's old fire station, replaced with a more modern structure at Civic Way. Not many years ago many houses in the Swadlincote area began to sink and crack because of subsidence and were held in place by wooden props.

Each year during the days of the nationalised coal industry South Derbyshire chose a Coal Queen to compete for the national title. These pictures show one of the local hopefuls setting off for the national final at Skegness.

Two pictures taken at the Swadlincote workshops of the National Coal Board. The workshops, and the Mining Research Development Centre at Bretby, played a vital part in designing, testing and developing new equipment to increase efficiency and safety in the mining industry.

The National Coal Queen, Miss Patricia Verey, of Burton Road, Overseal, was married at Overseal Parish Church to Mr Fred Smith of Mount Pleasant Road, Castle Gresley in July, 1975.

This 1988 picture at Bretby Stoneware works was taken when a Youth Training Scheme trainee had sleepless nights and refused to go to work. She claimed to have been terrified there by "a ghost".

What she heard and saw, it was thought, was the spectre of a turn-of-the-century tramp who slept for the night in a kiln to keep warm. Next morning it was bricked up and fired without anyone realising he was there.

Bricks from Bretby were transported to Egypt by Lord Caernarvon of Bretby Hall to form an entrance to the then newly-discovered tomb of Tutankhamen.

The clay industry scarred the landscape of South Derbyshire but brought employment and supplied a diverse range of products: pipes for sewage, toilet bowls, pots for the kitchen and table and art pottery.

These pictures of the South Derbyshire clay industry are from the archives of local historian Graham Nutt. This 1921 photograph shows a shot being fired at the Albion Clay Works in Woodville.

Baring the clay. That meant removing the overlying strata of waste material.

Clearing coal which had been blasted to expose the clay which would be used for making pipes for electric conduits, one of the many products of the Albion Clay Company.

The pug mill which mixed the clay.

Feeding clay into the machines.

Making Nineway conduits at the Albion works. There were also Tenway conduits, 10 pipes in one which could carry 10 electric cables. Thousands of pipes and conduits could be turned out in a day to meet the enormous demand in the early years of the century.

What connects South Derbyshire's clay industry with Alice in Wonderland? Thomas Goodwin Green, who in 1864 bought a Church Gresley pottery from Henry Wileman, was married to Mary, sister of Sir John Tenniel, who illustrated Lewis Carroll's famous story. Green built imposing new works which were destroyed by fire in 1904, the year of his death.

Putting the spots on T. G. Green's famous Domino Ware.

Making T. G. Green's even better-known Cornish Ware. George Smith, who had more than 40 years' service and became chief turner, is shown cutting the bands on the lathe.

How Cornish Ware jugs get their spouts.

The site of the former Mansfield Brothers pottery works at Main Street, Albert Village. In September, 1972, a petition was signed by 2,150 people against a scheme for a cement and blending plant there but they had to reopen the fight when the plan resurfaced the following April. The Rev D. Gibbons, leading the protesters, claimed fallout from the plant could affect the fabric of the church.

Gravel workings at Etwall. Extraction of gravel has played an important part in the economy of the areas around Burton.

Branston Chimney before demolition.

Silos at Steel Fabrications, an enterprising Burton firm.

Willington Power Station Open Day in 1972 attracted many visitors. Demonstrations of an asbestos fire protection suit and a beam engine made by apprentices proved just as interesting as the tour of the premises.

A rural industry at Tutbury has helped bring fame to the area. These pictures were taken when a new de-greasing machine was installed at E. B. and W. R. Chapman, sheepskin rug merchants, of Mill House, Tutbury, in 1979. Mr T. McGibbon (left) and Mr J. D. Chapman are seen treating a Canadian white wolf skin in the machine.

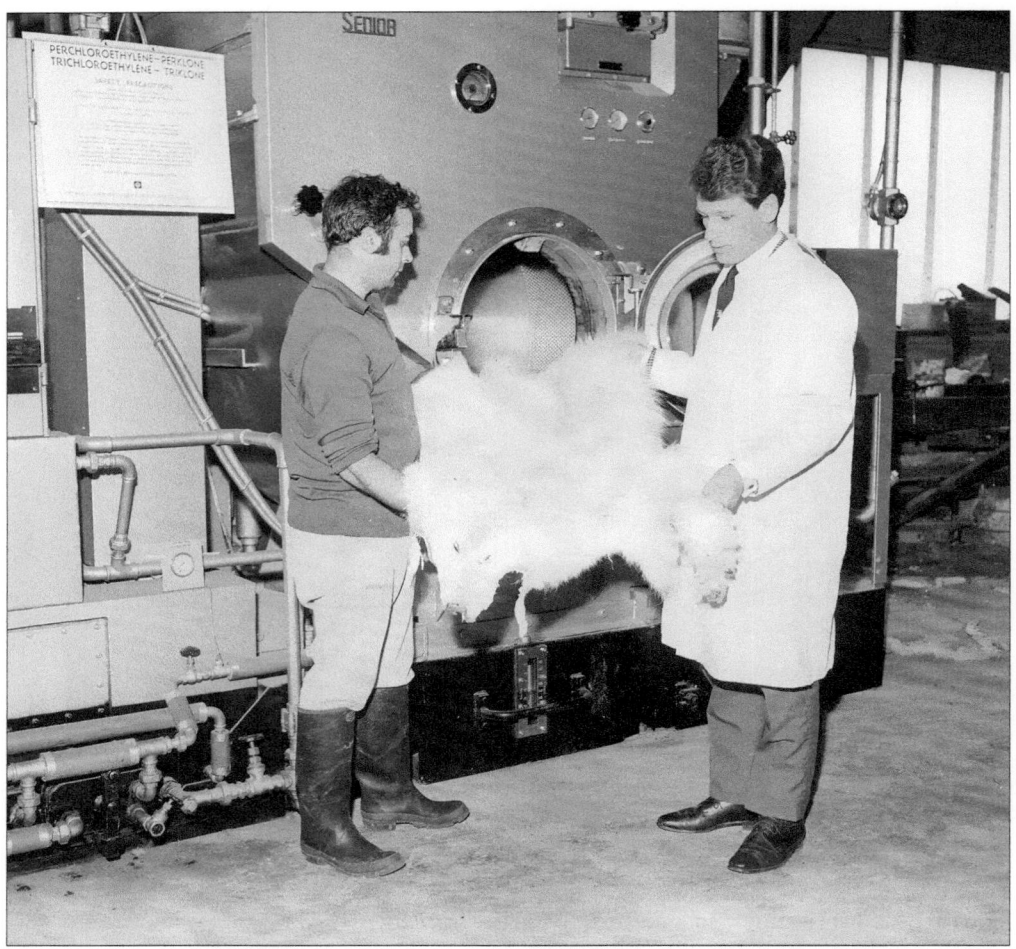

A £28,000, 45-ton diesel hydraulic loco left the Baguley-Drewery works in Uxbridge Street, Burton, in 1972 for the Republic of Korea. At the Chungji Fertiliser Plant it would work in extreme conditions varying from minus 20 degrees Centigrade (we hadn't learned to call it Celsius then) in winter to 40 degrees in summer, and the design and construction took this into account. It could haul loads of 1,600 tons. The firm was also busy building 12 seven-ton locos for Indonesia and eight large gearboxes for India as part of £1,240,000 worth of exports in progress at that time.

Sharp Brothers and Knight was an important timber firm in the town. The Sharp family were active in town affairs, including the Home Guard of the Second World War and the amateur dramatic societies which were a vital part of local life at one time.

A 1984 picture of the Co-op Dairy in Dallow Street. At first serving the needs of Burton Co-operative Society customers and then of the merged Derby and Burton Co-op, it was no longer needed after further amalgamations. In its day it not only dispensed fresh milk daily but was involved in manufacture of quality cheese.

Maltsters, coopers and other allied trades were kept busy by the Burton brewing industry. R. Peach and Co, malsters and barley merchants, had headquarters in Horninglow Street. They had maltings in Burton and elsewhere.

When John Farman, then 66, closed his Union Street basket making shop in 1975, it was the end of a family tradition going back 1,000 years. He made and sold baskets for 55 years; in Burton since 1953 when he took over the shop from the Toplis sisters. Mechanisation eventually made his time-honoured skills redundant, as has happened with other ancient crafts. He was originally from Norfolk.

The days before the First World War, when Il Duce, Benito Mussolini, was establishing his Italian empire, were when this picture was taken, showing rolls of newsprint arriving at the *Mail* offices in High Street. The building was the former town house of the Ratcliff brewing family of Newton Solney.

Many local firms can boast a good safety record and several have earned the right to fly a British Safety Council flag after a year without industrial accident. This shows the flag being proudly raised at Pirelli in 1975.

The Midland Joinery in Lichfield Street, Burton, and the adjoining remains of the long disused Bell's Brewery have been demolished and shops erected on the site. The man who built up the joinery business was the colourful Alderman Tommy Osborne, who chaired the town council's housing committee for many years, successfully wiping out the severe housing shortage of the time.

Sporting Heroes

The greatest day in Burton Albion's history. On May 9, 1987, the club made its first appearance at the famous Wembley Stadium, in the FA Trophy. A goalless draw with Kidderminster Harriers, also first-timers at Wembley, was followed by a 2-1 win for Harriers at The Hawthorns, West Bromwich. Nothing, however, could take away Albion's elation at appearing before a Wembley crowd. The picture shows Bob Gauden of Albion ("The Brewers") weaving through the Harriers defence at Wembley.

Dave Redfern of Albion gets his head to the ball on that memorable day on the world's most famous football ground.

Something to sing about: Paul Groves, Paul Bancroft, Neil Dorsett and Dave Redfern sing Albion's Wembley anthem assisted by the composer, Bernard Bagan.

Albion's Wembley line-up: (back, left to right) Brian Fidler (manager), Gil Land, Neil Dorsett, Clive Patterson (substitute), Nigel Simms, Steve Essex, Martin New, Dave Redfern, Ken Blair (assistant manager), (front, left to right) Paul Bancroft, Paul Groves, Joe Mulholland (trainer) David Vaughan, Dave Wood (substitute), Bob Gauden, Alan Kamara. These pictures of Albion's Wembley adventure are from Rex Page's book, *Burton Albion, Wellington Street to Wembley, The Complete History 1950-1990.*

Tom Bradbury, one time Burton Albion chairman, seen marking out the pitch. A local newsagent, he served the town as a councillor (it was his idea to have a municipal golf course) as well as a soccer director.

Burton Albion players pose with their Burton Albion Queen in October, 1975.

Albion's close neighbours and friendly rivals, Gresley Rovers, also made it to Wembley: in the final of the FA Vase (for the smaller non-League clubs) . A memorable game ended in a 4-4 draw with Yorkshire side Guiseley, who won the replay 3-1 at Sheffield United's ground.

One of Derbyshire's oldest football clubs (records go back to 1882), Gresley Rovers have played on the Moat Ground, Church Gresley, since 1909. In 1997 the club were champions of the Dr Marten's Premier Division but were denied their well-earned promotion to the Football Conference, because the Moat Ground was considered sub-standard.

Floods in Burton in 1875. The Plough Inn, though no longer a pub, is the only building on this picture remaining today. Thomas James Soar, who lived there, won a medal, pictured, when Burton Wanderers beat Burton Swifts in the Burton and District Association Challenge Cup final of 1886-87. He emigrated to America where his grandson, Thomas Soar, who recently moved from Massachusetts to San Diego, treasured it until burglars stole it. He visited Burton in 1980 to see where his grandfather had lived. Local soccer historian Ted Smith was able to give him a picture of his grandfather in that winning side (below).

There was a dramatic slump in Gresley's fortunes after this and, at the end of the 1998-99 season, the club were relegated to the Midland and West Division of the Dr Martens League.

Grandfather Tom Soar, an inside-forward, is on this picture of Burton Wanderers in 1886-87. The full line-up is: (back, left to right) R. Scattergood, G. Tunnicliffe, G. Chandler (captain), Mr Nice (president), A. Sheffield (goalkeeper), T. Black, W. Fellows, (middle, left to right) F. Burton, J. Parker (secretary), T. Soar, J. Bancroft, T. Bancroft (front, left to right) P. Murfin, M. Tunniclffe, W. Smith.

Grandfather Soar's medal.

Two of the best known footballers from Burton and district. Steve Bloomer (left) moved to the area at 17, signed for Tutbury Hawthorn, and went on to play for Derby County and England. Some say he was soccer's greatest player. Ben Warren, of Newhall, played for Derby County from 1899 to 1908 and Chelsea from 1908 to 1911, winning five North and South caps and 15 international caps.

The oldest Burton and District FA football picture showing Burton Excelsior FC in the 1872-73 season. It shows (left to right) H. Toon, H. J. Salisbury, H. Preece, A. Neale, J. Bould, H. Moore, Faulkner, J. Giltrap, W. C. Buxton, G. Wilson and R. Giltrap. The building has not been identified.

Three teams have represented Burton in the Football League. A team which began as Burton Outward Star in the 1870s became Burton Swifts in 1883 and were in the Football League Division 2 from 1892-93 to 1900-01. Burton Wanderers, founded in 1871, were in the Football League Division 2 from 1894-95 to 1896-97. The teams merged as Burton United, taking Swifts' place in Division 2 from 1901-02 until 1906-07, then failing to gain re-election after finishing 20th. Like the picture of Burton Wanderers (1886-87) on a previous page, this one of Burton Swifts in about 1890 was before the heady days in the Football League.

The last time a Burton side took part in the Football League: Burton United in 1906-07. Burton Town never made it to the League and, so far, neither have Burton Albion.

Wilf Watkins, a champion boxer for Burton Police as well as a keen footballer, is shown on this picture of the 1947 Lloyds FC line-up which won the Burton and District Challenge Cup that year, the second of three wins in succession. Back row (left to right): Arthur Marshment, Dick Plant, Stan Marshment, Appleby, George Burgh, Wilf Watkins, unknown. Front row (left to right): Fred Waltho, Matty Callanan, Midge Holland, Kes Gadsby, Bateman, Wally Phipp.

Tutbury Hawthorn also won the Challenge Cup in three successive years. The line-up for the third occasion, 1951-52, shown here, was: (back, left to right): H. Reynolds, referee S. Blencowe, E. Bostin, S. Billings (captain), L. Lewis, V. Haynes, S. Adams, J. Withnall, linesman T. Bradbury, R. Williams, secretary, (front, left to right) W. Hodson-Walker, D. Compson, P. Lewis, B. Hadfield, D. Cunliffe.

Tom Bradbury was later Burton Albion chairman and a member of Burton Town Council. A municipal golf club at Branston was his idea, but it later passed into private hands.

Phil Richardson, a member of the 1947-48 Netherseal St Peter's side pictured here and for many years an official of the club, later became the much-respected chairman of South Derbyshire District Council. The full line-up is: (back, left to right) T. Stone, F. Smith, R. Yates, G. Evans, A. Hill, K. Ball, T. Bradford, (front, left to right) Phil Richardson, E. Homer, G. Redfern, Dennis Stone, D. Lord.

Burton and District FA representative side has brought honour to the town in regional competitions. Making up the 1965-66 team were: (back, left to right) W. Wilson (Newhall United), A. Bailey (Burton Albion), B. Parks (Midway Amateurs), F. Tomlin (Midway Amateurs), K. Brown (Technical Old Boys), R. Seaman (Pirelli), (front, left to right) Green (Stapenhill), A. Taylor (Gresley Rovers), D. Bentley (Winshill), P. Hall (Gresley Rovers), E. Salt (Robirch).

Grange Street Football Club, 1947.

Peter Taylor (right), who made his name in League football as a goalkeeper, had his first job in soccer management with Burton Albion before going on to achieve unprecedented success with Brian Clough at Derby County. He is pictured with Ted Smith at the launch of Ted's book marking the centenary of Burton and District Football Association, of which Ted was general secretary for many years.

Football's first Knight, Sir Stanley Matthews, on a visit to the area in 1973, pictured at the Riverside Inn, Branston.

Before the Second World War most Burton schools played Rugby football, through for some years afterwards only the Boys' Grammar School did so. This pre-war picture shows a team at Christ Church School when they beat the holders, Stapenhill, by 11 points to nil in a schools' competition. On the left is headmaster Mr "Socker" Thompson and on the right Mr "Daddy" Everett. The boys are (back, left to right) Phipps, Ted Smith, Hunt, Spalding, Tipper, C. Smith, Sherratt, Taylor, White, (middle, left to right) Holland, Parry, Joyce, Stone, (front, left to right) Paley, Scott, Mason.

Jack Baker, a local policeman who played for Burton (Rugby Union) Football Club for many years before the Second World War and again afterwards, captained this 1949-50 side which played 36 games, winning 20, losing eight and drawing eight, gaining 400 points with 229 against.

In the side are Bill Souster Junior, who later ran the Baguley Engineering Company in Uxbridge Street, and Percy Davies, who became sports master at Burton Technical High School. Lining up for the camera are: (left to right, back) H Fawkes, K. Roberts, K. Tunley, G. Thomas, J. Turner, R. Franklin, L. Watts, J. Roach, (middle) M. Upton, L. Rees, W. Souster, J. Baker (captain), P. Davies, L. Wilcock, E. Morris, (front), M. Jones, R. Wood, N. Tomkins, H. Redfern.

The club was founded in 1870. The brothers Frank and Herbert Evershed (later Sir Herbert) were outstanding players in the 1880s, Frank becoming the town's only international, playing forward for England several times. Herbert nearly made it, being an England reserve. This picture shows four early stalwarts of the club, A H Yeomans, G. T. Barker, Frank Evershed and Herbert Evershed.

One of many high spots in the club's history came when it won the Staffordshire Cup in 1972-73. This group includes C. Wady, I. Roberts, S. Gotheridge, J. Hunt, J. French, W. Stephenson, B. Langlsow, R. Wadsworth (capt), J. Warren, P. Davies, I. Birch and D. Sunderland. Missing from the picture is R. Brooks.

A shot of the pavilion at Peel Croft, headquarters of Burton (Rugby Union) Football Club. There have been many improvements to the ground's facilities since this picture was taken about a quarter of a century ago.

Mark Osman, a Boys' Grammar School boy, captained the England under-15 Rugby team in 1973. They drew with Wales at Cardiff Arms Park and then won at Twickenham. His brother, Russell, played soccer for Ipswich Town and England and their father Rex was on Derby County's books. Rex was licensee of the Bull's Head at Repton and was later involved with Burton Albion Supporters' Club.

The Allied Breweries Sports Ground at Belvedere Road was for some years used by Derbyshire CC for at least one county cricket match each summer. The club, variously known when run by the brewery as Allied and Ind Coope, is now a private organisation known as Belvedere Sports and Social Club, membership no longer being confined to past and present brewery employees.

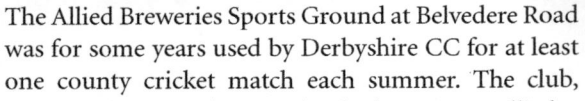

Near the River Trent, the Bass Cricket Ground has also seen some action, as on the occasion of this 1975 clash between Derbyshire and Oxford University.

A Burton Leander Rowing Club four, racing at Burton Regatta just before winning the Wyfold Cup at Henley Regatta in 1958. The crew comprised (right to left), bow Lionel Street, 2 Colin Pritchard, 3 George Lawson, 4 Brian Chamberlain.

Outside Burton Leander Rowing Club's boathouse, the President, Mr W. E. C. (Bill) Souster, is presented with the Wyfold Cup by stroke George Lawson on the crew's triumphant return from Henley in 1958.

When long-serving Mr W. E. C. (Bill) Souster retired as president of Burton Leander in 1963 the club commissioned a portrait of him. Admiring it are (left to right) Mr John Jennings MP, Mr Harold Harding and Mr Bill Souster junior.

Members of Burton Leander RC on a club outing to the Fish Pond Hotel, Matlock, in 1919. Those shown include (left to right): 1 Keggy Cumper, 2, Reg Wyatt, 4 J Hadfield, 7 Jack Auber, 8 George Beesley, 11 Ralph Ashton, 12 R Clements, 13 Reg Crabtree, 15 G Franey, 16 Harold G Harding, 18 Eric Waite, 20 Walter John Mason, 23 Frank Wellings, 25 Ralph Beesley, 26 Jim McDonald.

The christening of a Trent Rowing Club boat. Like Burton Leander, the club has brought honour to the name of Burton at regattas throughout the country.

Jack Bodell of Newhall won the National Coal Board amateur championships, then turned professional in 1962. He outpointed Joe Bugner at Wembley to win the British, European and Commonwealth heavyweight titles. Later he sparred with "the greatest", Mohammed Ali.

The inevitable choice to declare open Swadlincote's Greenbank Leisure Centre was Jack Bodell, who more than anyone had put "Swad" on the map.

Jack, having won and then twice successfully defended his British title, was awarded the Lonsdale belt and brought it back to show to his greatest fans, the people of South Derbyshire. Here a huge crowd on the Delph at Swadlincote cheers his achievement. Behind Jack is the famous "Time the Avenger" clock on Swadlincote Town Hall.

Jack tries out the equipment at the Greenbank.

You can't win 'em all. Jack lost twice to Henry Cooper, in 1967 and 1970.

Neville Brown, a second cousin of Jack Bodell, was a successful Burton amateur boxer before turning professional. He too won the Lonsdale Belt, becoming the longest-reigning middleweight champion in British boxing history.

Weightlifter Tony Ford took part in the 1972 Olympics and later won a gold medal for Britain at the Commonwealth Games in Christchurch, New Zealand.

Power lifter John Humble built up an impressive array of lifting records over the years, then started again notching up veteran records. Later he ran health and fitness clubs, first in the former Burton Museum, then in Uxbridge Street and later at the Imex Centre in Shobnall Road.

Burton Athletic Club at the annual athletic meeting on Peel Croft in the 1936-37 season. Those pictured are: (back, left to right) Harry Stocks, Harry Blood, Jack Gould, Arthur Ormerod, Jack Sharpe, Alex Wileman, (front) Ted Smith, Doug Haynes, Ernie Gold, Len Foster, Dennis Foxon.

Bert Gibbs, for 28 years a machine minder at the *Burton Mail* in a department producing house magazines for local industries, had a spectacular bowls career .

He played 11 finals of Burton and District Crown Green Bowls Association Individual Merit contest and won nine of them, in 1932, 1933, 1948, 1949, 1950, 1951, 1958 and 1965. He won the South Derbyshire Individual Merit in 1934 and Doubles in 1956, the Wyggeston Challenge Cup in 1971 and Derbyshire Qualifying Merit competition in 1973. He played for Winshill most of his life and had spells at the Punch Bowl (1948 to 1951) and Working Men's Club.

His father, another Bert, joined Winshill in 1908. By the 1930s nine members of the Gibbs family played for the club. Later the younger Bert's sons, Ivor and Trevor, played alongside him. Ivor and his son, Richard, are still playing.

This view of the Albion Hotel at Shobnall as it was in the mid-1960s shows the bowling green, which has now given way to a children's play area. The bowls club started in 1887, five years after the pub was opened. Some other local greens have been taken over for car parks or housing, but the game still flourishes in Burton area.

Leading members of Shobnall Bowls Club, based at the Albion Hotel, in the late 1970s. The picture shows: (left to right) Malcolm Cheese, club treasurer and treasurer of Burton and district Bowls Association, Maurice Dolman, chairman, John Jones, Graham Jones, Albert Dukes, George Banton and John Mander.

The centenary celebration at the Stanhope Arms Hotel, Stanhope Bretby, was also a very special occasion for Charlie Tooby of Outwoods Street (extreme right). It was his 90th birthday, so although he did not take up bowls until he was 50, he had clocked up 40 years of bowling. Chairman Maurice Dolman (centre) presented him with a special award for being the longest-playing member.

Kevin Kent, who provided these pictures of Shobnall Bowls Club, and who was its secretary, is third left. Jim Eccleshall (third right) owned the New Street business, Midland Fertilisers. He was the club groundsman and brother of Burton Albion's groundsman, Tom.

Alf Claber, who defied the march of progress by riding round Burton in a pony and trap in the 1970s, was licensee of the Albion Hotel and later of the Bridge Inn at Branston. He is seen (right) presenting the Claber Trophy to Graham Jones.

The traditional opening of the season. Bob Andrews, who was free trade director of Marston's Brewery, starts things off for Shobnall Bowls Club. Bob had been regimental sergeant major on Field Marshal Montgomery's staff during planning of D-Day and worked closely with him after the invasion of Normandy.

In the days of Burton County Borough, bowls contests between police and town council were an annual feature. This is one of the last, in 1972. Another traditional fixture was the match between teams fielded by the mayors of Burton and Derby.

Burton Golf Club inter-club foursomes in May 1969. The old established club at Bretby (its third home) was for some years the only one in the area. What began as a Burton municipal golf club was later established at Branston and has been developed beyond recognition under later private ownership. There is also a thriving club at Craythorne near Stretton.

Burton Golf Club Ladies' Day in 1975.

Trophies displayed in 1973 at Burton Judokwai, one of several martial arts organisations in the Burton area.

The cycle speedway craze hit Burton in the 1950s and there were several local clubs of enthusiastic youngsters taking part in the new sport. One of these was Burton Whirlwinds, pictured in 1951.

The River Trent at Burton, home to swans and other waterfowl, has enriched the town's life by providing a venue for rowing, speedboat racing, angling and, in the years before people knew the word pollution, swimming. Water-skiiing has also been seen on the Trent from time to time as these three pictures show.

Raft races have also provided plenty of fun on the Trent. This shot shows a Venture Scouts raft race. For several years the Technical College Students' Union raft race drew huge crowds but doubts about the cleanliness of the water led to it being discontinued.

It is claimed the game of water polo was originated in Burton, which sadly has no water polo team now. This Burton team in the 1950s comprises: (left to right, back) Bill Kirkham, M. Howe, Arthur Benton, Rees, (front) Bill Mayger, Gould, John Hilton.

Successful local angler Tony Scott at Walton. For some years he ran a fishing tackle shop in Burton.

It must have been the only time that a locally owned racehorse reached the heights when, in 1997, Lord Gyllene won the Grand National. Millionaire tycoon Stan Clarke, of Barton-under-Needwood, bought the horse for a song (comparatively speaking) in New Zealand. The village of Barton was bedecked with flags and bunting and hundreds turned out to cheer when Lord Gyllene was paraded through the streets after the Aintree triumph.

Members of Burton Sub-Aqua Club taking part in a game at Burton Baths in 1973.

A keep fit competition at Swadlincote's West Street Darby and Joan Club in 1973.

Darts has always been a popular game in the pubs of the area. This picture shows a dinner of Burton Ladies' Darts League at Burton Drill Hall in 1969.

Scenes Old and New

The 12th-century Burton Bridge was the scene of a Civil War battle in 1321. A new, straighter, bridge was built in 1864 but parts of the old bridge remained standing for years. This and several other pictures in this book are from the collection of Mr Len Foster, who worked in Burton Gas Showrooms and was promoted to manager at Derby and then Lincoln.

This 1903 postcard by Jackson's of Burton shows a handsome structure on the corner of Guild Street and Horninglow Street, built as offices for the Town Commissioners. It was used by Burton Borough Council from 1878 until Lord Burton presented the present Town Hall in 1894.

Later the old building was replaced by mundane but functional offices for the Transport Department which ran the town's buses. Now the later building is used by Staffordshire Trading Standards Department.

Cars and buses, including this product of the Ryknield Motor Company, were once built in Burton. Baguley Cars and Salmon Motor Company were other local manufacturers. The town was once seriously considered as the site for the Rolls-Royce car factory, but lost out to Derby.

The 150ft spire of Christ Church, built in 1844, had to be removed as unsafe after the 1944 Fauld explosion. It was the second disaster to hit Christ Church. In 1916 a Zeppelin bomb destroyed the adjoining mission room, killing a woman preacher and injuring other people. Nowadays the Anglican parish has been merged with that of All Saints and Christ Church is used by the Elim Pentecostal movement. The Caribbean Club stands on the site of the Mission Room.

Near Holy Trinity Church is shown the only railway level crossing in Britain to have three sets of gates, because of the width of Horninglow Street. The railways linked with Allsopp's brewery near the Hay, Allsopp's cooperage and Horninglow Station.

Holy Trinity Church, rebuilt in the early 1880s because of fire damage, was demolished in 1973. Between it and the one-time council offices on the corner of Guild Street were the premises of a blacksmith, cab owner, wheelwright, drug and herb stores, servants' registry office, fishmonger and cork manufacturer. Until 1924 this part of the street was used for the October horse fair.

In the foreground of this picture of Burton Market Place are Chippy Heap's fish and chip stall and, with striped awning, Ronde's ice cream barrow. Premises on the right have been replaced by Abbey Arcade. Farthest away is the Man in the Moon pub, where the Town Commissioners met. Then comes Brown's the butcher's, Draper's, who sold glass and china, Thomas Oliver's meat display and Povey's refreshment rooms.

Laying the tram lines in Station Street in 1903. One the corner is the Wheatsheaf pub, later replaced by the Fifty Shilling Tailors and then John Collier's ("the window to watch"). Six or seven decades later policemen still referred to "Sheaf Corner", though few of them knew the reason. The area is now pedestrianised.

On this site St George's Hall was built as a theatre in 1867. From 1902 the Opera House there was used by local and visiting operatic companies. Sometimes music hall acts were presented, and on these occasions the theatre called itself the Hippodrome. It was replaced in 1934 by the Ritz Cinema which was to become the Odeon and latterly Robins.

You could buy margarine at a shilling (5p) a lb at the Maypole shop in Station Street before the First World War.

Claymills Sewage Pumping Station, which served Burton for many years, now preserved by enthusiasts.

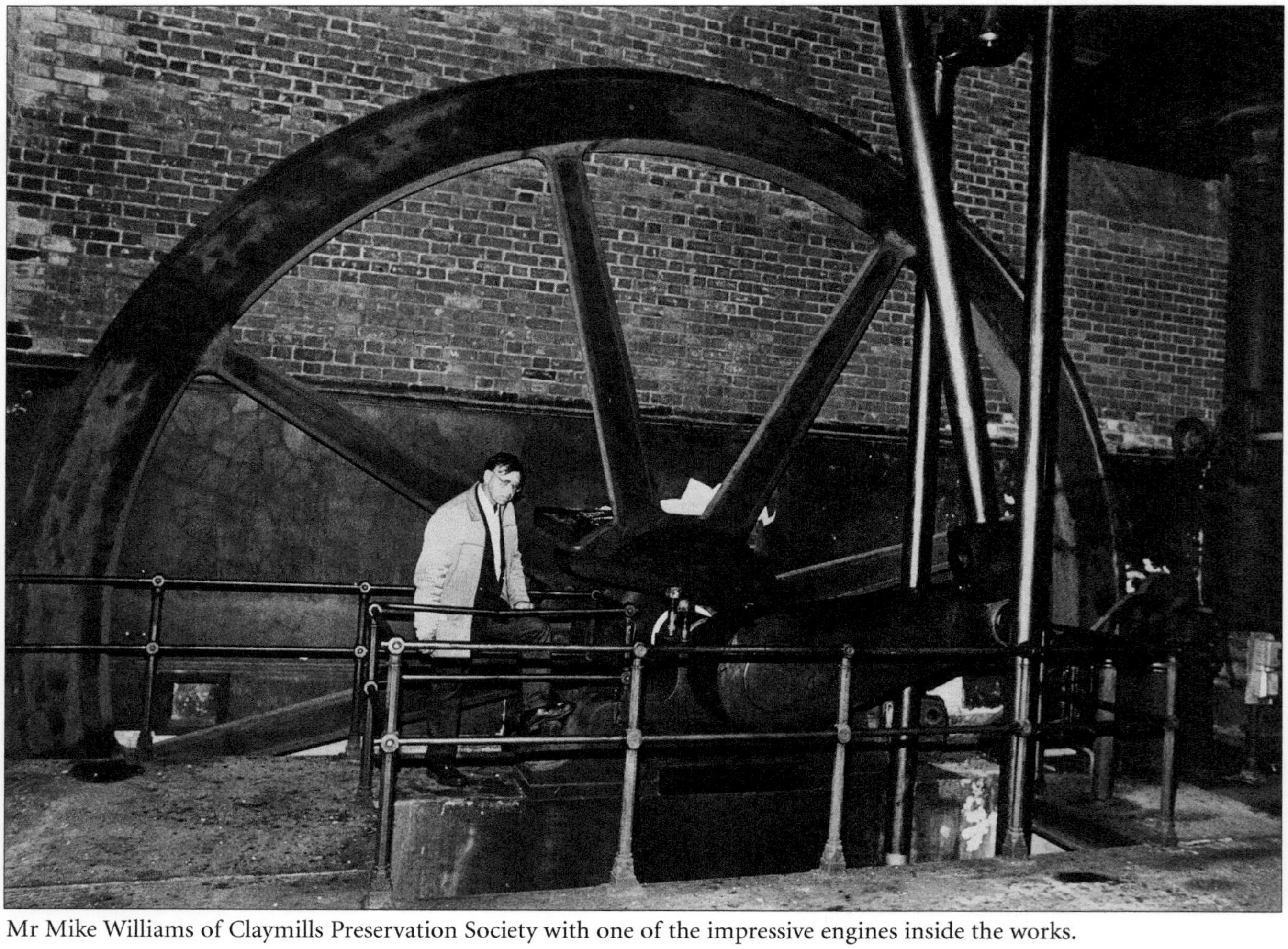

Mr Mike Williams of Claymills Preservation Society with one of the impressive engines inside the works.

At the junction of High Street and Horninglow Street there stood for many years a number of oak posts. The originals were there that so when horse-drawn wagons negotiated the corner they would not hit pedestrians or buildings. Thus the junction became known as The Bargates.

To the confusion of some people asked to "meet me at the Bargates," the name was given to Burton's first shopping precinct, a little way down High Street from the junction. Since then, however, it has changed its name to Riverside Centre and, mercifully, that hideous frieze has been discarded.

The Burton Cooper statue, paid for by Burton Civic Society and individual donations, was first erected at the High Street end of St Modwen's Walk, one of the malls in the central shopping centre. Unveiled in 1977, this sculpture by James Butler, is a reminder of a craft that once employed many Burtonians but had virtually ceased to exist. It became a useful rendezvous point and an unofficial symbol of the town.

From the precinct's opening, in the late 1960s, shoppers were unprotected from rain and wind.

There was outrage when new owners of the precinct claimed the statue as their own and resited it inside the shopping area, which they renamed Cooper's Square. Somehow the larger than life figure seems dwarfed by its present surroundings.

In the 1990s the precinct was roofed over and doors provided at each entrance so that shoppers in what is now Cooper's Square are untroubled by the elements.

Details of some of the upper stonework on a building in Guild Street, Burton, once the offices of the School Board and later of Burton Education Committee. Adjoining was Guild Street School, closed as a school in the 1940s, its building being used for additional education offices and the Little Theatre. Now the combined buildings are used by a carpet firm.

This building on the corner of George Street and Guild Street in Burton was originally the Liberal Club, later George Street Club and in recent years has had various business uses.

Alderman Charles Tresise, whose family, originally Cornish, owned a printing firm in Burton and founded two local newspapers, laid the foundation stone for the lead-domed magistrates courts in Horninglow Street, Burton, in 1910. Seventy years later a more modern court building was erected alongside it.

Burton Civic Society, responsible for many schemes for enhancing the town, opened an arboretum near Stapenhill Church in 1990. The president, Mr Jim Lloyd (left) is pictured with retired engineer Mr John Ploughman at the ceremony.

Another picture at the opening of the Arboretum. Adults shown are Mrs Olga Lloyd (with walking stick), Mrs Valerie Burton, and Mr John White, then East Staffordshire Council's head of leisure.

Main Street, Stapenhill, showing an old town dwelling with an even older tree fronting the roadway. Pictures like this are used by Burton Civic Society to encourage local people to become more aware of their environment and to support preserving the best and improving the rest.

The Greyhound Boat Club Rally at Horninglow Basin of the Trent and Mersey Canal in 1986. Once loads of beer and coal were carried by canal barges to, from and through the town. Now there is a constant stream of pleasure boats.

The Horninglow Canal Basin, now overshadowed by the A38 flyover, was brightened by a colourful wall mural and the planting of a garden.

Volunteers at work on the canalside garden.

Their work was given a civic send-off by Councillor Peter Haynes, chairman of East Staffordshire Council and a former Mayor of Burton.

Almshouses in Hawfield Lane, Winshill.

Another view of Hawfield Lane shows the School Hall and House in 1984. St Mark's Church was the gift of John Gretton, of Bass, Ratcliff and Gretton the brewers.

These Victorian almshouses in Wellington Street, Burton, were originally built for 20 poor women. The Town Hall clock can be seen in the background.

Diagonally opposite, Wilkinson County Stores was THE place to shop for several generations, but this store, offering quality and personal service, was to expire with the dawn of the supermarket age. The premises are now occupied by Jackson's Motorcycles.

Magg's and Butt's shops in Waterloo Street, Burton, on the corner of King Edward Place, were demolished to make way for the council offices in 1939, adjoining the already existing, and more ornate, Town Hall building.

Just a few yards further along Waterloo Street was Roe's Motor Garage and Pit, a busy place when many people cycled to work and the more adventurous and better off were beginning to buy cars.

Just long enough ago for people to suggest that the Victorian terraced housing in Uxbridge Street, Burton, could be enhanced by tree planting. Try now, and the number of parked and moving cars would defeat any such notion. In the distance can be seen the block containing Burton General Hospital wards. The hospital was demolished in the 1990s and houses built on the site. Also in the distance can be seen the tower of Christ Church, which lost its spire as a result of the Fauld explosion of 1944.

The public library building in Union Street, Burton, was for many years too crowded to accommodate the books, let alone the many additional facilities that more modern libraries were able to offer. Years of campaigning by Burton Borough Librarian Mr Kenneth Stanesby led eventually to construction of a spacious replacement off High Street.

Probably more people knew where to find the Leopard Inn than this humble place of worship very close to it: the Friends' Meeting House, headquarters of Burton's Quakers.

Pictured in the snow, a sculpture of a Viking longboat fashioned from wood and stone which forms part of the Burton Sculpture Trail. It can be found at the Ox Hay, near where an arm of the Trent, much used for swimming before the days of pollution, was filled in when the main river was dredged in the 1960s.

A former grain warehouse in Burton beside the railway has become the offices of East Staffordshire Borough Council's planning department.

A civic send-off for one of the town's first municipal trams, which set off from Wellington Street for Bridge Street. Coming into service in July, 1903, they began to be replaced by motor buses in 1927 but some still ran for another three years.

The Burton and Ashby Light Railway Company also rans trams in Burton, heading for Swadlincote and Ashby. The 80-minute journey from Burton to Ashby or vice versa cost 6d (2.5p) and was known as the Sixpenny Switchback. There was one fatal accident, in October, 1919. The brakes failed on one of the company trams causing it to run backwards down Bearwood Hill Road, Winshill, and overturn. Conductress Lilian Parker and a woman passenger died and l6 people needed hospital treatment.

One of the Burton and Ashby Light Railway trams at Hill Street, Swadlincote.

The first Burton Corporation bus, a Guy single-decker.

Double deckers, some of them eight feet wide, had to be introduced over the years because of the huge number of passengers. Then, when the austerity of the Second World War and early post war years ended and car owning became widespread, the Corporation transport system had to be subsidised by the ratepayers instead of paying its own way.

A Burton Corporation double-decker bus decorated to mark the end of the County Borough in 1974. Burton had been a municipal borough from 1878 and then a county borough from 1901, running trams or buses for 71 of the 73 county borough years.

The Bass sign above the Swan Hotel was a familiar landmark at the end of the Trent Bridge for decades until big brewers were compelled to sell off some of their pubs and Kimberley's took over. There is no truth in the legend that The Swan owes its name to being on the junction of roads leading to Stapenhill, Winshill, Ashby and Newton Solney.

Above and right: From the dawn of the 20th century Burton people were aware of the need for a second bridge over the Trent and by the time it opened in 1986 the old bridge was frequently congested with local and long-distance traffic. These two pictures show the parade which formed part of the celebrations when St Peter's Bridge opened.

Burton bridge was the scene of a Civil War battle and appropriate dress was worn when this plaque was put in place in recent times by Burton Civic Society.

Road works at Branston in 1967 when the Burton Bypass was constructed. As a result the A38 carrying traffic from Birmingham to Derby no longer needs to go through Branston and Burton but housing, shopping and other developments mean the older roads are still very busy.

The Abbey Inn, with its riverside lawns, in the centre of Burton. The building, though modernised throughout the centuries, was once the farmery (hospital) for the monks of Burton Abbey.

The Abbey Club, popularly known as the Gentlemen's Club, comprising well to do members of Burton society, had sole use of it for many years, but for the last few years it has also housed an inn providing meals and licensed refreshments in pleasant surroundings.

Not far away, on the wall of the Cooper's Square shopping centre, the history of the abbey is displayed for the benefit of townspeople and visitors.

The Abbey Gates pictured in 1927 before demolition. A fault on this picture much amused local historian Mr H J (Jack) Wain. Had the camera picked up the ghostly shade of one of the old monks?

The bandstand in Stapenhill Recreation Ground attracted music lovers and courting couples before and during the Second World War. Local brass bands, and visiting bands, entertained. Changes in people's habits and musical tastes spelled the end for the bandstands — there was also one in Outwoods Recreation Ground — in the post-war years.

Each year the Statutes Fair in the market place and parts of adjoining streets enlivens the town centre of Burton. Once it was an occasion for hiring farm labourers and servants for the coming year. In modern times the dodgems, ghost train, big wheel and other amusements vie for the support of fun-seekers.

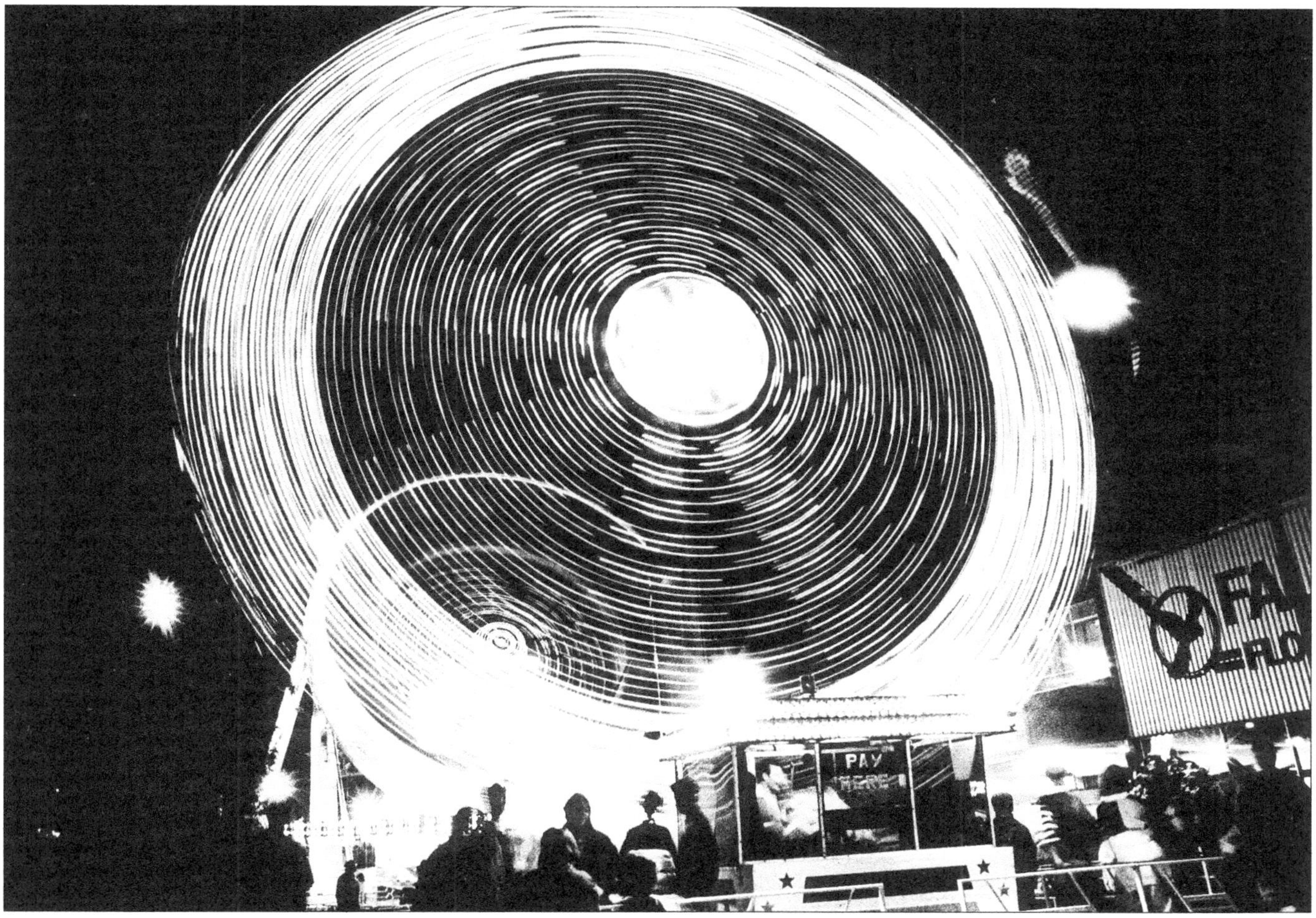
PAY
HERE

LEOPARD INN
Marston's
CANDY FLOSS
SWEETS
SUPER FROGGIT GAME

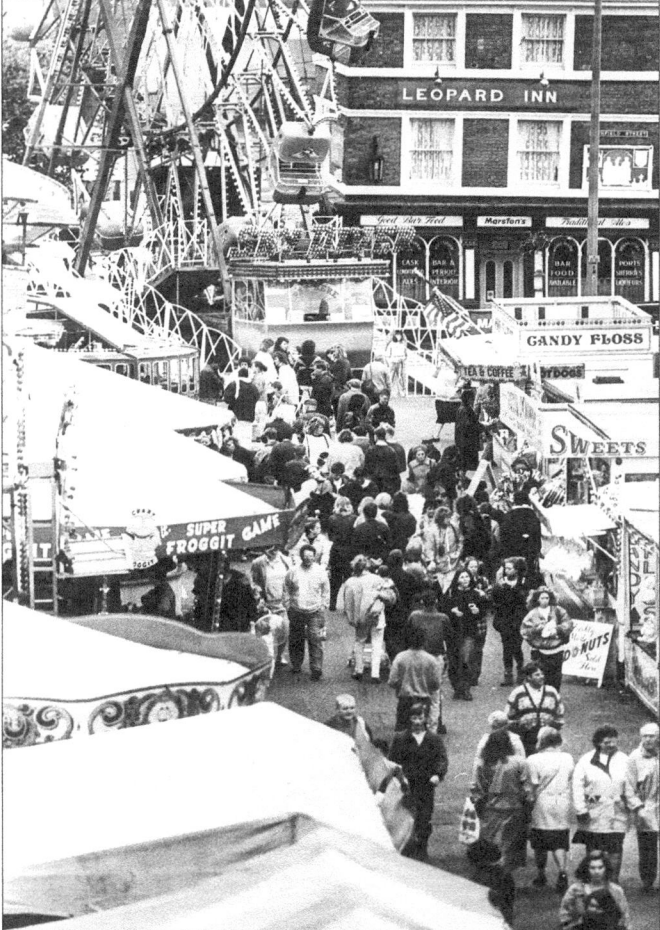

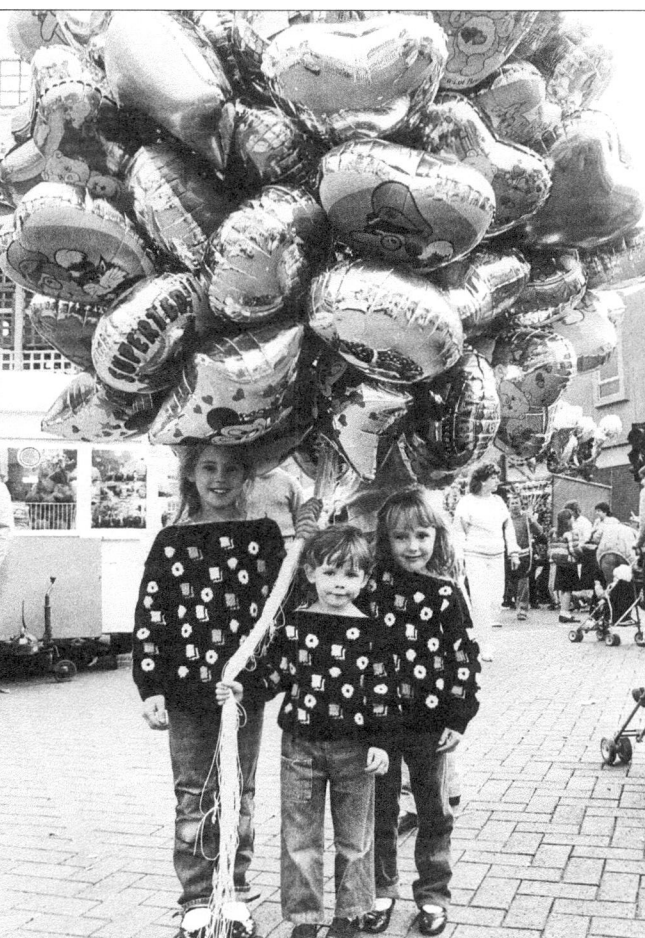

A horse-drawn bread delivery van of Burton Co-operative Society outside Tunley's Dairy in Shobnall Street, Burton. The petrol shortage during the Second World War and for a time afterwards delayed the replacement of these once familiar vehicles by more modern means of transport.

The Soho, an old house beside the River Trent, demolished to make way for the Technical College (now Burton College). In days when the river was navigable as far as Burton there was a wharf there for loading and unloading Burton ales, timber, iron and other commodities.

At one time there was not much more than a "Bobby's Button" and a couple of swings in Burton's Cherry Orchard, but now there is a variety of children's play equipment.

Another view of the Trim Trail, in 1983, showing Councillor Stan Deeming, then chairman of East Staffordshire Council, giving the enthusiasts a civic send-off.

The Trim Trail on the Burton Meadows provides the opportunity for varied exercises for those minded to Keep Fit.

The less energetic can follow the Sculpture Trail on the Meadows. This wind sculpture depicts St Modwen, the Irish Saint who first brought Christianity to the town.

The Old Fleet Stones, not far from where now the Ferry Bridge and Viaduct provides a river crossing at Burton. Both pubs have gone, and so has the Burton brewery of Bindley and Co which supplied ales to one of them.

The Wyggeston Hotel on the corner of Foston Avenue and Calais Road, Burton. Its name, and that of Wyggeston Street, derives from an investment in land in that part of Burton by a Leicestershire family from Wigston.

The Royal Oak in Newton Road, Burton has long been popularly known as "the Sump Hole" and is a popular venue for local sportsmen and for those who enjoy a glass of beer beside the river. The old buildings of Greensmith's Flour Mill can be seen in the background.

Inside Greensmith's. Miss Carolyn White at the first break of the cereal.

A closer look at Greensmith's Flour Mill. Part of it dates back to at least 1745. Thomas Greensmith bought it in 1889 and part of his business was grinding corn for wholewheat flour, being promoted by Sir Oswald Mosley of Rolleston. A wide range of animal foods was produced by the firm, which made use of steam-powered road vehicles in the early years of the 20th century.

The packing floor.

Patrick Watts with a stone grinder.

One of the firm's vehicles.

The latter days of Greensmith's.

Local planners took a keen interest in the flour mill when the business closed. There was talk of an industrial museum there, but the idea was not mentioned when proposals were made in mid-1999 for flats.

Burton Infirmary, later General Hospital, has now been demolished and replaced with a small housing estate. Before the National Health Service it was partly supported by modest weekly contributions from a large number of local people who thereby qualified for free treatment when required. There were also annual church collections.

The Trent near the mill is a good place for fishing for those entitled to make use of it.

The old fire station in New Street, Burton, was replaced by one in Moor Street in 1973, one of the last major schemes of Burton County Borough. The New Street building was converted into a motor showroom for TL Darby in 1979, and thus a local landmark was preserved.

Another view of the old Fire Station in New Street. For more than 120 years Burton was responsible for its own fire brigade but in 1974, on local government reorganisation, it became part of the Staffordshire Fire and Rescue Service.

The new fire station in Moor Street nearing completion in 1972.

Across the road from the old fire station is the former Burton Head Post Office. It was one of those closed in the late 1980s, and people now draw their pensions and buy their licences at a local supermarket.

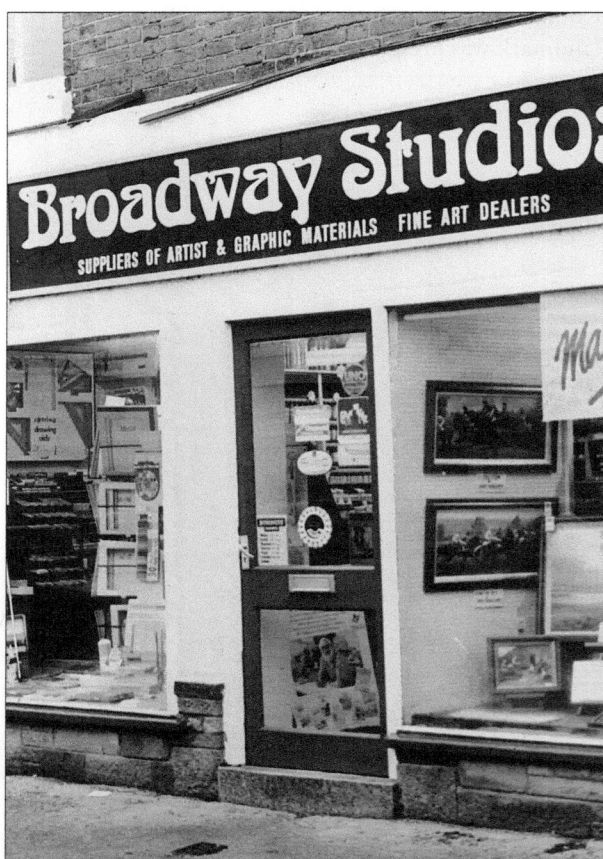

This New Street art shop, now closed, is remembered only by the older generation as the Crown public house, but younger people can still recall when it was a cafe.

When this picture was taken in 1965 the High Street end of New Street was a busy shopping area. The building on the corner had been a cycle shop and a car showrooms and was a cleaners at the time of the photograph. The Dog and Partridge pub, whose landlords had included former Derby County player and ex-Burton Albion manager Jack Stamps, a sweet shop, cafe, newsagent's, another pub, antique shop, union office and other businesses are among those in view. All have gone now.

An important brewery engineering firm in Burton for many years has been S. Briggs and Co, which took over the older established Thornewill and Warham in 1929. Its Moor Street premises were demolished in 1969, and later the New Street premises (above) would go to make way for the Octagon Shopping Centre. The firm, subject eventually of a management buyout, continues in the former Robert Morton-Delaney Gallay works in Derby Street.

A 1965 view of the other end of New Street. The chemist on the right has gone. So has the General Hospital on the left. The railway level crossing is now a dim memory, but the adjoining urinal is preserved at the town's Bass Museum.

The Bass Shires, stabled at the Bass Museum, join shoppers in part of the Cooper's Square precinct.

A fireman's house adjoining the old New Street fire station was later converted into a restaurant.

This 1956 picture of Cyclists Touring Club members from Burton and elsewhere gives an impression of the grandeur of the old railway station building, later replaced with a less imposing structure.

A famous local photographer of the past, Richard Keene (Breedon Books has published a volume devoted entirely to his work) took this picture of Burton's Ferry Bridge in 1900.

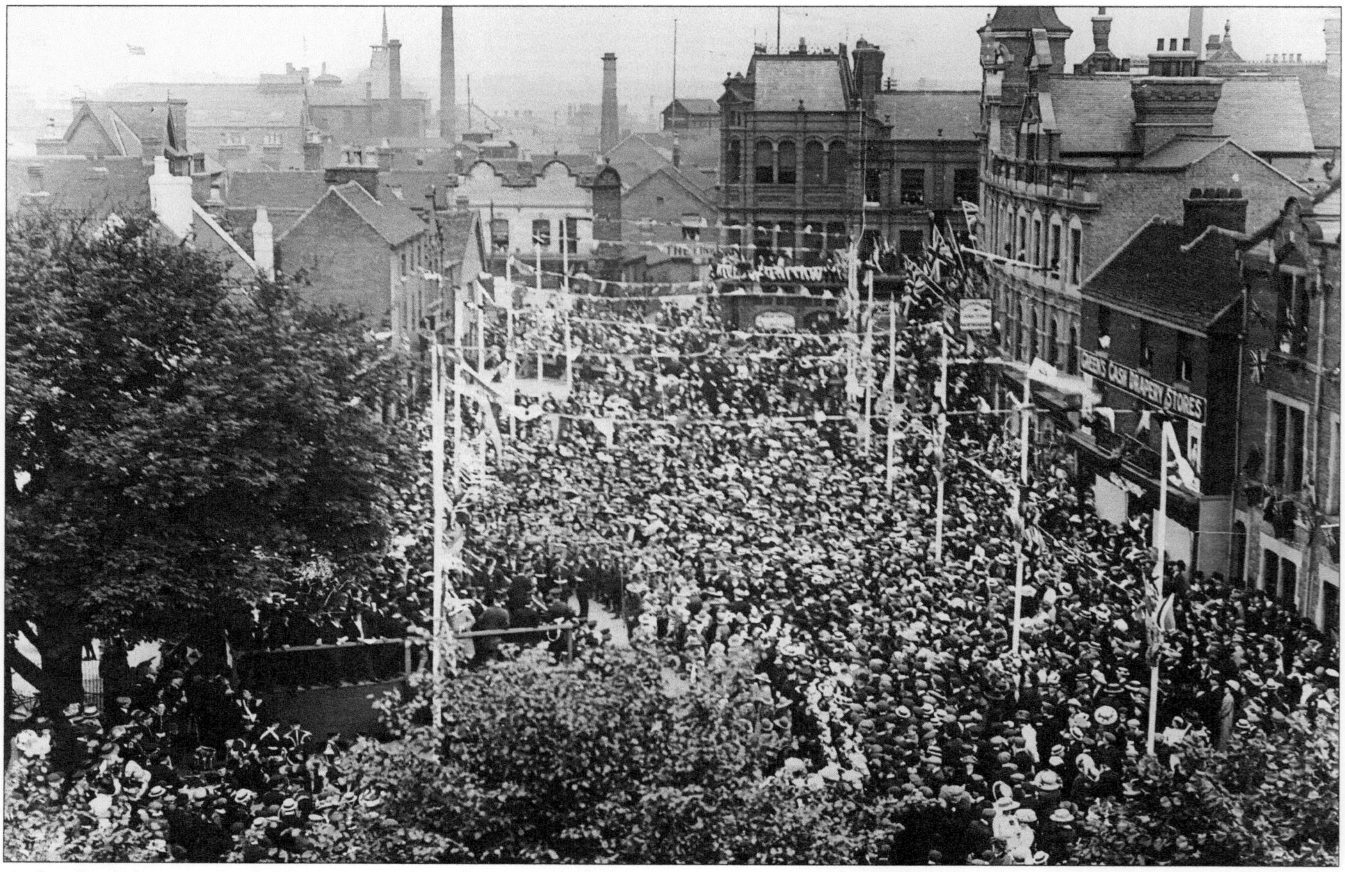

A thanksgiving service in Burton Market Place to mark the end of the First World War. This picture, taken from the tower of St Modwen's Church, shows in the background buildings now swept away by redevelopment.

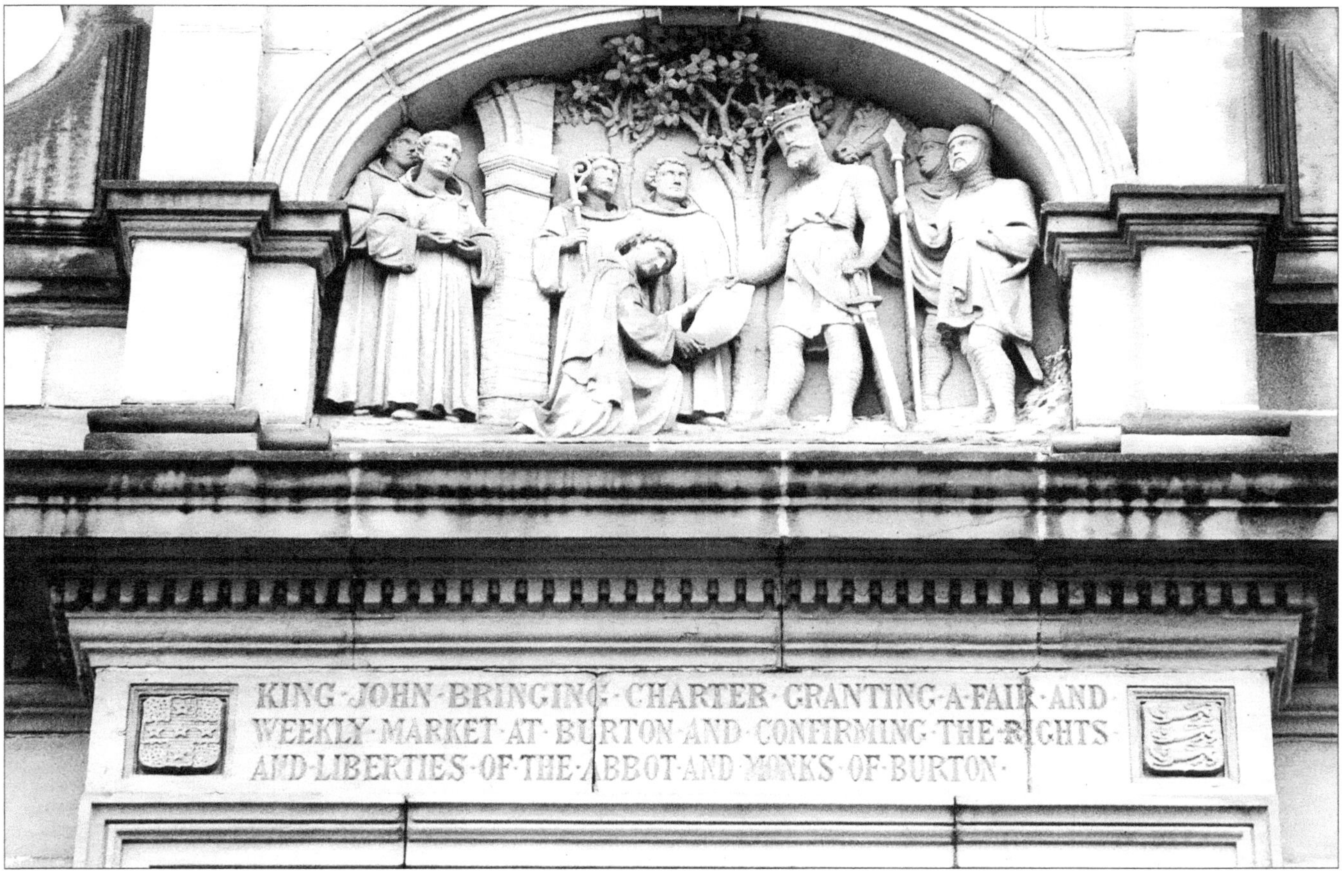
KING·JOHN·BRINGING·CHARTER·GRANTING·A·FAIR·AND·
WEEKLY·MARKET·AT·BURTON·AND·CONFIRMING·THE·RIGHTS·
AND·LIBERTIES·OF·THE·ABBOT·AND·MONKS·OF·BURTON·

This representation of an 11th century event in the history of Burton can be seen above one of the entrances to Burton Market Hall.

ROYAL OAK
Lounge

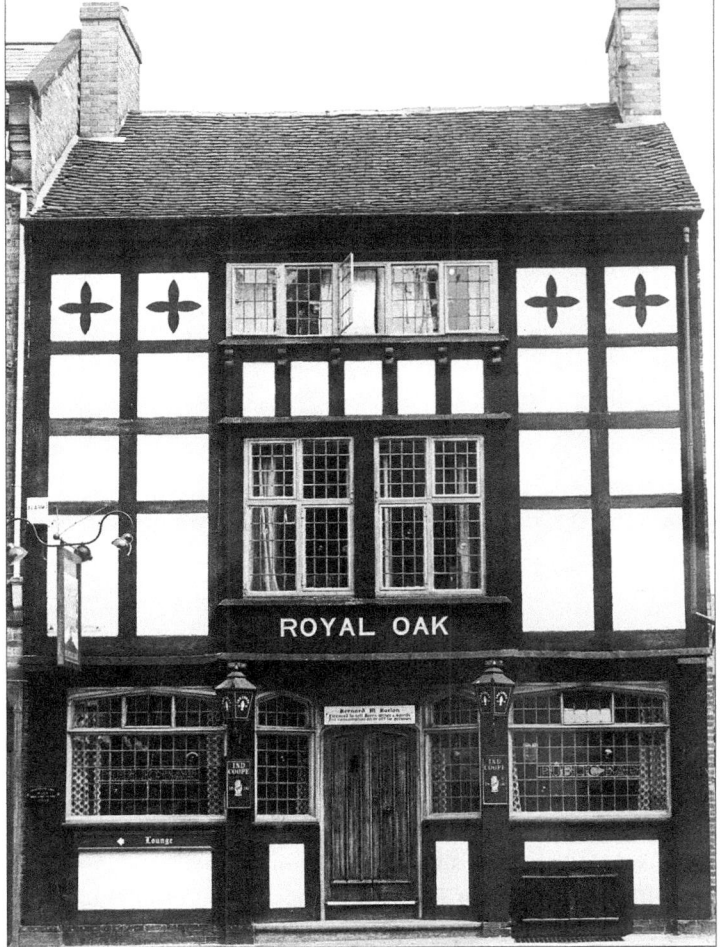

The pub in the Market Place which is reputed to have housed the town lock-up where the local constable, Dick Roe, who himself enjoyed a snifter, would incarcerate drunks or wrongdoers.

The one-time joiners' shop of the Bass brewery in Horninglow Street, Burton, has been converted into a museum of brewing which attracts huge numbers of visitors every year. The museum also includes an experimental brewery and the stables of the famous Bass Shires.

The Bass Museum attracts tourists from all over Britain and abroad. This exhibit is the Worthington White Shield bottle car, once a familiar sight on the streets of Burton and on promotional visits to other towns. The 1992 picture shows museum curator Mrs Sarah Elsom and museum administrator Mrs Rachel Challen.

Metal urinals like this were once a feature of Burton's street scene until well after the Second World War. They were long ago replaced by more hygienic conveniences but this one was preserved by the Bass Museum.

The combined newsagents' and sub-post office on the corner of Guild Street and Horninglow Street, Burton, opposite the magistrates' courts, together with the adjoining shops and offices in Horninglow Street, was swept away with the development of the Bass Museum.

This imposing building in High Street, housing an automobile showroom and other businesses, was among those demolished to make way for the central shopping precinct, later known as Cooper's Square.

Next to it was Bank Square where stood the White Lion pub, a tobacconists, an ironmongers' and a jewellers'. Beneath the Progressive Supply Company can be seen the windows of what was once Pearks' grocery store.

Construction of the shopping precinct meant the controversial demolition of a 16th century building, the Dame Paulet almshouses, which had long served as the local weights and measures office. The unusual carving over the doorway, perpetuating an error by a not-too-literate stonemason, is now preserved in the wall of Littlewoods' store.

High Street, Burton, in 1912, taken from near the junction with Station Street. The ornate frontage of the Electric Theatre added to the allure of Burton's first purpose-built cinema, for which the architect was Thomas Jenkins. As Mayor of Burton, he declared it open in 1910. In the latter half of the century it was closed. The tram lines dated from 1903.

Another old view of High Street, looking towards the Electric Cinema, shows, on the left, the White Hart Hotel where, in Edwardian times, farm workers were hired for a year at the time of the Statutes Fair and carriers loaded on market days to carry goods to local villages.

Station Street is very different now, with its building society offices, charity shops and its pedestrianisation scheme. The building just before the now demolished Methodist Church (with spire) was Tarver's clothing store, above which Ted Smith lived in his childhood. There was living accommodation above most shops half a century ago.

A closer look at Tarvers, where Irish Menswear now stands.

Stapenhill church seen from Alligator Point. Ted Smith says that this area was the playground for himself and other children from the town centre. It was also a good place for swimming before the Trent became polluted by the march of industrial progress.

An old view of Woods Lane, Stapenhill, from a glass negative in the *Mail* archives.

The cemetery at Stapenhill Road, Burton. The spires denote the two chapels used at one time for funeral services.

Another view of the Ferry Bridge linking Stapenhill to the town centre.

Before the Ferry Bridge opened in 1899, people paid a penny a time to be rowed over the Trent between Stapenhill and the town. Even afterwards, they had to cross the muddy meadows until the Stapenhill Viaduct was added to the bridge.

A busy scene in Station Street, Burton, showing horse drawn carts and the tramlines.

Burton's Market Hall, built in 1883 and modernised in 1938, was once much busier than today, with stalls all round the balcony as well as at floor level.

The old town hall in Burton Market Place, used by the Town Commissioners before the days of town councillors.

The Town Hall before King Edward Place was laid out and the adjoining council office block built.

This ornamental urn was long a feature of Stapenhill Pleasure Gardens until someone stole it, apparently not in admiration of it for they threw it away. It was later found damaged and enthusiasts restored it and put it back on show.

Mr Tim Watts looking at the 1856 board detailing tolls to be paid for crossing the bridge with animals or carriages at the bridge over the river at Walton-on-Trent.

In the 1940s the old bridge was replaced by a Bailey bridge constructed by Army personnel. At one time the rattle of the wooden surface as cars drove over it could be heard a mile away. Improvements over the years have done away with the noise.

Not far from the Bailey Bridge is the Walton village church, dedicated to St Laurence.

The church gateway.

Another Walton landmark, the Shoulder of Mutton pub.

Fires and Firefighters

The biggest fire in Burton's history was that of February 24 and 25, 1954, which completely destroyed the Ind Coope and Allsopp hop store and contents. Damage was estimated at £750,000. This picture shows the devastated store.

A group of firefighters involved in tackling the blaze.

Nine firemen, including Chief Fire Officer RC Elliott and Deputy Chief G. McCoy, needed hospital treatment, six overcome by fumes and three with eyes badly affected. All appliances of the town fire brigade and the brewery's own brigade, assisted by contingents from Swadlincote, Derby, Tutbury, Leicester, Staffordshire, Derby and Derbyshire, fought the fire. The Bass brigade stood by at the fire station in case of any other calls in the Burton area.

As this aerial view shows the three-storey building between Station Street and Brook Street was closely surrounded by other structures. The bricked-up windows made ventilation difficult, and the three entrances were unusable because of smoke and fumes. The internal railway system created additional difficulties for fire fighters.

There was another big fire at Ind Coope in 1962 involving the number 3 malthouse. One problem was the large oil tank nearby.

A bridge between numbers 2 and 3 malthouses was damaged by the fire.

A police officer thought he smelled burning in the early hours of a Sunday in 1966. He peered through the windows of New Street Baptist Church but saw nothing: because the building was smokelogged. Still suspicious, he roused the caretaker. Before she could unlock the church its roof blew off. The officer dashed to the nearby fire station. By then flames were leaping high in the air. Burton, Bass and Ind Coope fire brigades fought the fire and Swadlincote firefighters stood by to cover the rest of the town.

The basement boiler had been left ticking over during the night and the wind caused a blowback starting the fire, which quickly ate through the wooden floor of the church.

Heat was so intense it melted the plastic blue lights on the fire engines and portable radios in the windows of the Union Street nurses' home opposite. The high wind fanned the flames and the church was gutted, only the walls left standing. It had to be demolished and now the Comet electrical goods shop stands on the site.

Not only the official town fire brigade but a number of brewery brigades contributed to the safety of the town until after the Second World War. They helped each other when there was a big blaze. This picture from an old *Mail* glass negative shows the Bass Fire Brigade.

Miss Cinderella (Carol Entwhistle) at the Burton Fire Brigade Field Day of 1969.

The Green Goddess fire engines, which for some years were kept at the former Branston Central Ordnance Depot and later moved to Marchington, were brought into action during a nationwide strike of firefighters.

Among Young People

The Friars' Walk school building, an 1830s replacement for the older building on the site which had been the birthplace of Burton Boys' Grammar School three centuries earlier. The Grammar School moved to Bond Street in 1877 and to Winshill in 1957, but the Friars Walk building has remained well used for educational and church activities.

A 1922 picture reprinted in the *Burton Mail* half a century later led to a revival of Guild Street School Old Boys' Association. A reunion dinner was held in the Midland Hotel in February, 1973. The school closed in 1940 but its former scholars continued to sing its praises for a lifetime.

Paget School sports on the Clarence Street playing fields in Burton in 1975. The Paget School on Burton Road, Branston is the successor to the old Anglesey Secondary Modern School in Clarence Street, itself descended from Clarence Street elementary school.

The final of a schools debating contest organised by Burton Junior Chamber of Commerce.

Two pictures of a South Derbyshire schools sports meeting 22 years ago. Hard work by teachers in and out of school hours contributed to the success of such events and encouraged young people to keep fit and to give of their best in competition.

Victoria Road School.

A team from St Edwards Roman Catholic School of Newhall, Simon Ashby, Brian Johnson, Teresa Regan and Paul Cavanagh, won the Swadlincote Accident Prevention Council junior inter-schools road safety quiz at Springfield Road School in Swadlincote in 1973.

Remember the slogan Plant a Tree in '73? A group of Anglesey School pupils from Burton did just that, at Repton.

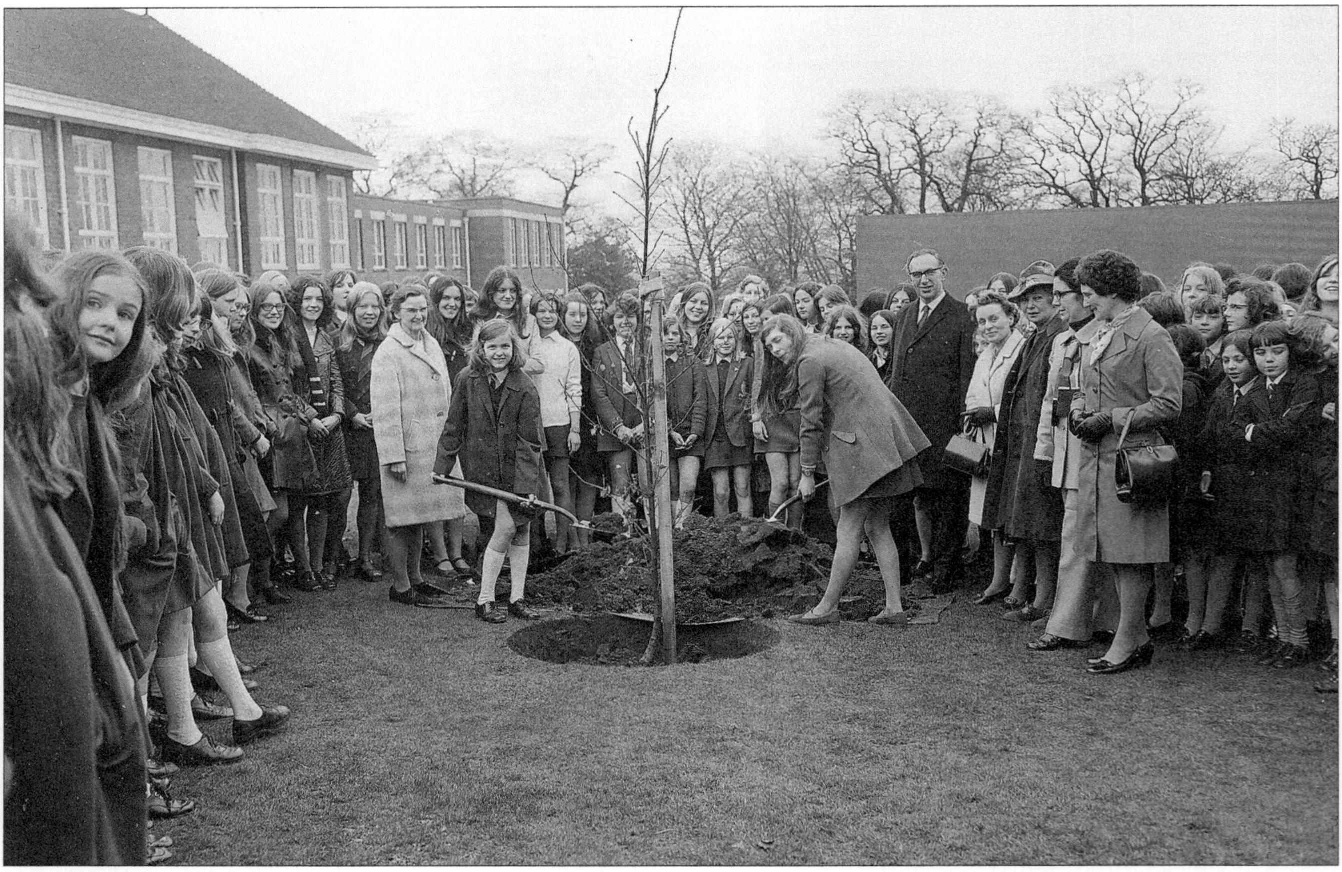

More tree planting, this time by pupils of Burton's Girls' High School, who chose to do it in their own school grounds at Winshill.

Burton's Girls' High School Old Girls beat the school 3-1 in a hockey match during the school's centenary weekend in 1973. Both teams are shown here. Other events included an exhibition of old photographs and uniforms and a dinner. The school began as Allsopp's Girls' High School in Waterloo Street in 1872. The foundation for the new school at Winshill, now part of Abbot Beyne School, was laid in 1926 and the girls moved in there in 1928.

This model of a Concorde was made at Horninglow Secondary Modern School, an example of education keeping up with the times.

May Day celebrated by youngsters of the Edge Hill Playgroup in Stapenhill in 1973.

Above and opposite page: At the annual speech day of Granville School, Woodville, in 1972 headmaster Ronald Evans reported that there were 500 pupils and this would increase to 800 by September, 1973. Hillary House was awarded the shield for best house at the Granville speech day that year.

Safe cycling trials at Pingle School, Swadlincote, in 1972.

A speech day of Anglesey Secondary Modern School, forerunner of Paget High School. The Anglesey School building at Clarence Street is now a junior school.

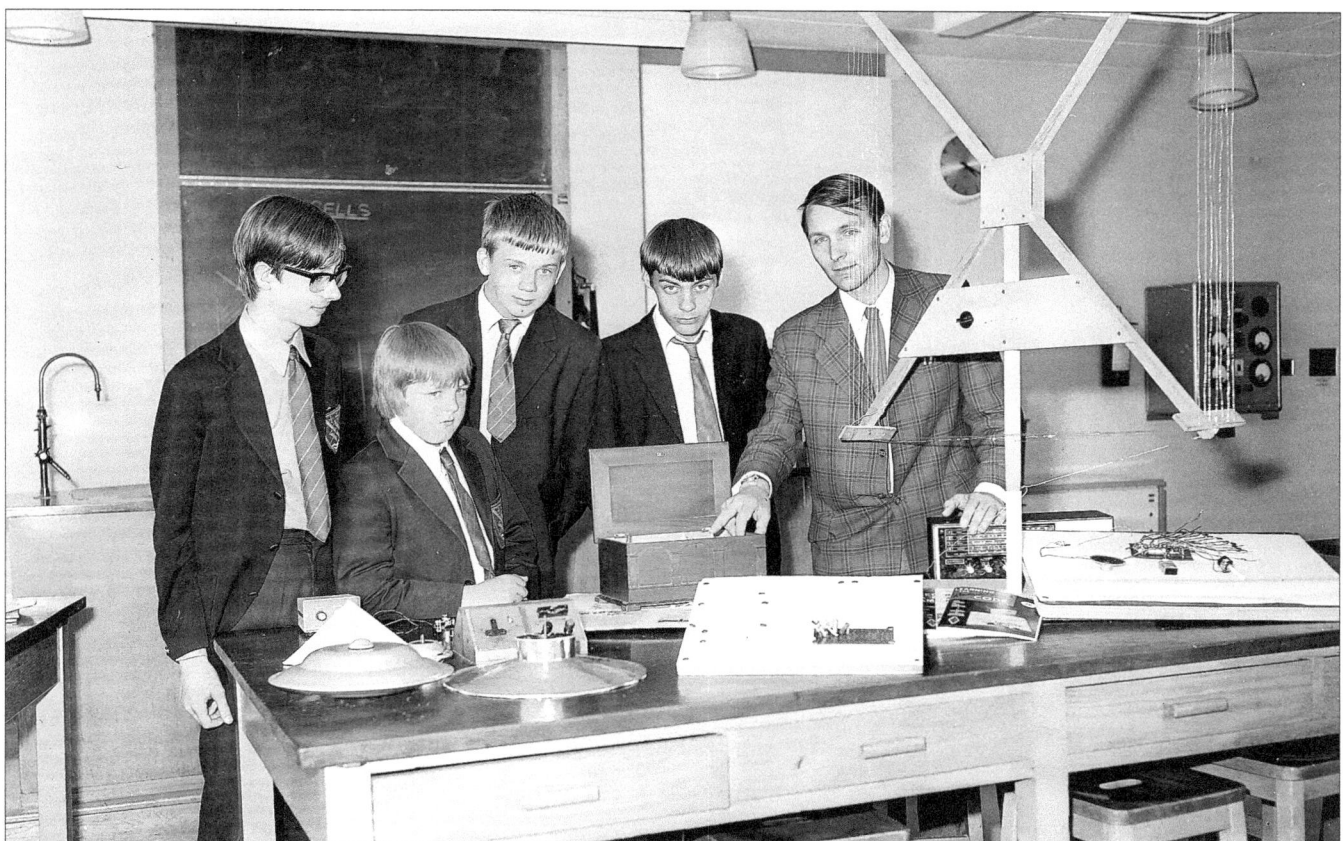

Before the Second World War the emphasis in schools was on the three Rs. In later years the scope widened, as this reminder of a 1975 science project at Winshill's Ada Chadwick School tells us.

The 3rd Burton Wolf Cub pack in the early 1930s. The Scouting movement has played a prominent part in the lives of young people throughout Burton, South Derbyshire and adjoining areas.

The Church Lads' Brigade unit based on Burton Parish Church in the late 1930s. On the left of the back row is Charlie Long of Stapenhill and on the right of that row Ted Smith. In the middle of the centre row is Captain Walter Dudgeon, a gas fitter known to his friends at the gasworks as Sludge Pump. On the right of that row is Sam Parry, whose parents were caretakers of the museum on the corner of Guild Street and Station Street. A gas fitter before the Second World War, Sam was also a trumpet major in the Staffordshire Yeomanry. He served in the Western Desert with the Yeomanry and was then commissioned in another regiment. After the war he became a teacher at Clarence Street School until he retired.

Sponsored walks, swims, silences and other events have raised money for good causes in Burton and South Derbyshire in recent years, and we met a couple of Newton Solney schoolgirls who walked round their village in custard-filled wellingtons not long ago. This sponsored swim by Repton Scouts, Guides, Cubs, Brownies and Venture Scouts in July, 1975, was to raise money for a new headquarters.

The Duke of Edinburgh awards scheme has been well supported from the start by schools and youth organisations in Burton and South Derbyshire. These 1975 pictures show an awards ceremony at Burton's Girls' High School.

The Festival of Queens, held annually for many years in Burton Town Hall, was an occasion when girls chosen by Methodist Sunday Schools throughout the area gathered together, each bearing the money collected in their Sunday Schools for the National Children's Home. This 1973 picture shows some of the queens and their attendants.

Members of the Air Training Corps 351 Squadron leaving their headquarters in Horninglow Street, Burton, in 1972 for a week's camp at RAF Machihanish, Argyllshire.

Church Gresley Cubs set off for a camp in 1975.

Six Burton boys attempting to beat the Peterborough 100-hour marathon record for table soccer in 1972. Taking part were Graham Harrison, Brian Gill, David McKorman, Peter Brown, Chris Brindley and Nick Jackson.

A St John Ambulance cadet social in Burton in May, 1969. Both Burton and South Derbyshire have a good record of support for St John Ambulance.

Burton Sea Cadets, housed in a former Burton Leander boathouse renamed Training Ship Modwena after Burton's patron saint, has won numerous awards for smartness and efficiency. This shows an inspection of the Sea Cadets in November, 1972.

Children, supervised by their parents, try things out for themselves at a toy exhibition at St John's Hall, Horninglow. The event was part of National Playgroup Week in 1969.

A children's party at Rolleston Commemoration Club in 1973.

A Modern Miss contest at Burton Town Hall in 1975 was part of East Staffordshire Council's programme of entertainments for children. Over the years the council has widened its scope of activities to provide fun and learning for both children and adults.

Spotlights, Footlights

Cyril Glover started his first band in Burton at the age of 15, going on to play in the RAF Central Band and then professionally with the famous Bert Ambrose and Sid Phillips Bands. He could play clarinet and saxophone, sometimes adding a comedy routine in which he played the xylophone with his feet at the same time as belting out a tune on the clarinet. He formed his own band which toured the Mecca Circuit and appeared on TV, then ran a resident band at the Savoy Hotel in Guernsey. He died in 1998, aged 81. The picture shows him fronting his Burton band at Burton Drill Hall around 1937. At the back are Len Nash, double bass, Jim Shaw, drums, and Stanley Walters, piano. In front (left to right) are an unknown page boy and Bill Pitt, Ben Silk and Douggie Stimpson (later with Eric Winstone's Band), saxophones, Joe Fearn, guitar and accordion, Randy Draper, trumpet, Harry (Chick) Williams, trumpet, and Penny Redfern, vocalist. Len Nash, Joe Fearn and Randy Draper later ran their own local dance bands.

Burton musicians honour the memory of one of the town's most famous sons, nationally known organist Armsbee Bancroft, who earlier played piano in local dance bands and ran a resident quartet at the Stanhope Arms Hotel, as it was then known. Among those playing at the Memorial Concert are: (left to right) Len Nash, double bass, Freddy Lawrence, piano, Jimmy Baxter, keyboard, Joe Fearn, guitar, Don Hughes, drums, and Roy Norton, saxophone.

Burton Theatre Arts Ball, organised by Fred Warren of one of the town's many amateur drama companies, was a popular annual event at the Town Hall for many years. There was keen competition for the prizes for best fancy dress costumes, and even the musicians wore colourful garb. Here we see Joe Fearn's band at the ball in 1960: (left to right) Pete Wilkins, vibraphone, Cliff Collier, clarinet, Maurice McCann, saxophone, Norman Willey, drums, Ben Silk, saxophone, Max Margetson, guitar, Horace Bunting, bass, and Armsbee Bancroft, piano, with Joe conducting.

One of Burton's best remembered dance band leaders, Len Reynolds, at Swadlincote Rink, a popular dance venue, just after winning the Midland Dance Band Championship at Smethwick in 1945. The line-up includes his son, Tony, and the world famous drummer, Phil Seamen.

Mr Arnold Pennington of Chorley, who served as a teacher at John Taylor School, Barton-under-Needwood, and William Allitt School, Newhall, took this picture of Newhall Town Band on the steps of Hammersmith Town Hall in 1964, on the occasion of a contest.

A later picture of Newhall Town Band, which has a proud history in contests and concerts. It has also recorded albums, on one occasion with vocals by comedy actor John Inman.

Burton Operatic Society, founded in 1886 and still going strong, used to appear at the Town Hall and then at the Opera House, later to be a cinema, in Guild Street. For many years now it has appeared mainly at what was Horninglow Secondary Modern School, and is now part of de Ferrers High School. This picture was taken in 1972 when rehearsals were taking place at Stapenhill for a production of Princess Ida. The musical director was Mr Arthur Ormerod, who was assisted by Coral Gould. Evelyn Woodhouse was accompanist and the title role was taken by Sheila Boyce.

Another picture of Burton Operatic Society, this time rehearsing for a *Songs from the Shows* presentation in Burton Town Hall in 1973.

Presentation of a cup at a drama festival in Burton Little Theatre in 1973. Although the Little Theatre in Guild Street no longer exists its name is still proudly borne by the Little Theatre Players, whose productions are now more likely to be seen at Burton Brewhouse Arts Centre.

The Queen's Theatre in Wetmore Road attracted variety acts to Burton before the Second World War, during which it provided a social centre for American servicemen. It was demolished soon after this 1987 photograph.

Burton has been fortunate in a wealth of amateur talent. At one time there were the Argosy Players, Trent Players, Jubilee Players and other groups. One of the strongest was Burton Shakespeare Society, seen here rehearsing *The Two Gentlemen of Verona* in Burton Little Theatre in 1973.

A former brewery building in Duke Street, used by Bass at one time as laboratories, was converted to provide the town with a much needed facility, the Burton Brewhouse Arts Centre, which can be used for theatre productions, dance tuition, exhibitions, a variety of art and crafts activities and much else.

The Rita Chambers School of Dance, one of several highly reputable organisations of the kind in Burton and district, rehearsing for *Pot-Pourri,* a show it was to present at Dovecliff Grammar School, Horninglow, in 1972.

Giant pipes awaiting disposal after Burton Town Hall organ was dismantled in 1972 to make way for a Wurlitzer, which people now travel miles to hear.

The Wurlitzer, although new to Burton, had seen service in a Manchester theatre.

Times Past

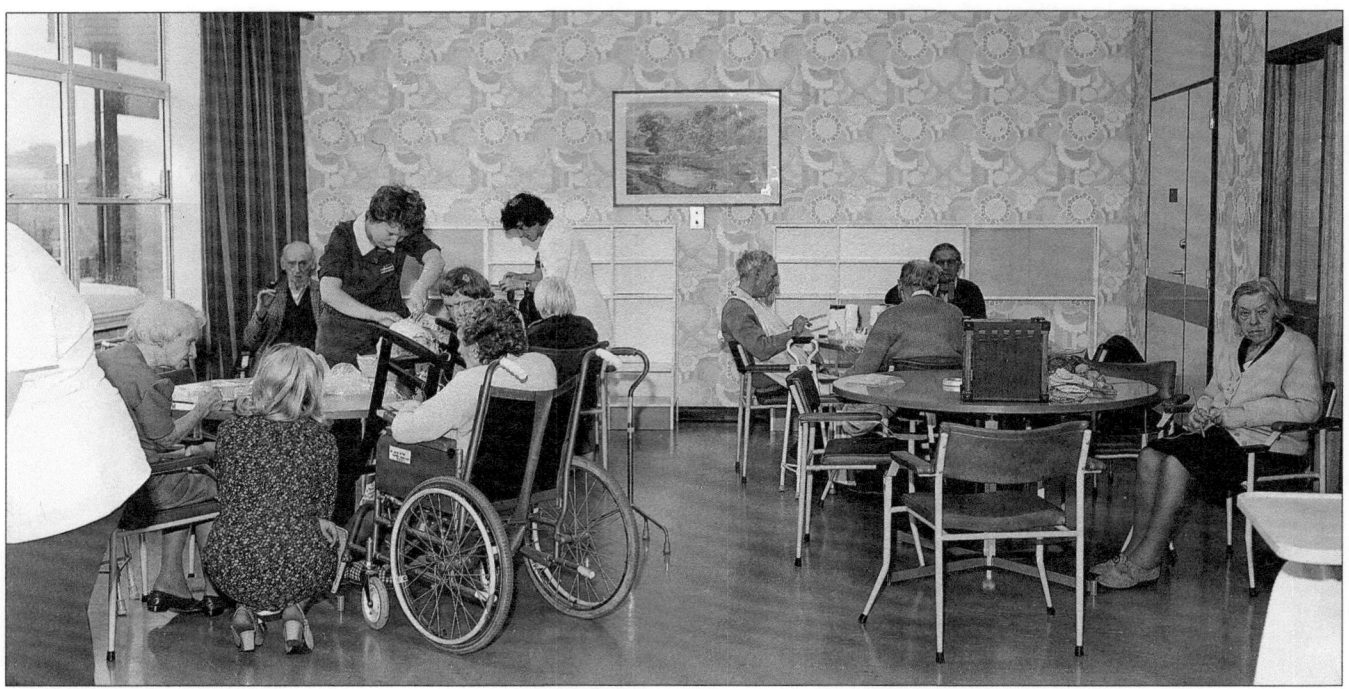

The Geoffrey Hodges Wing of Burton District (now Queen's) Hospital was opened in September, 1975, and since then has provided care for many elderly people.

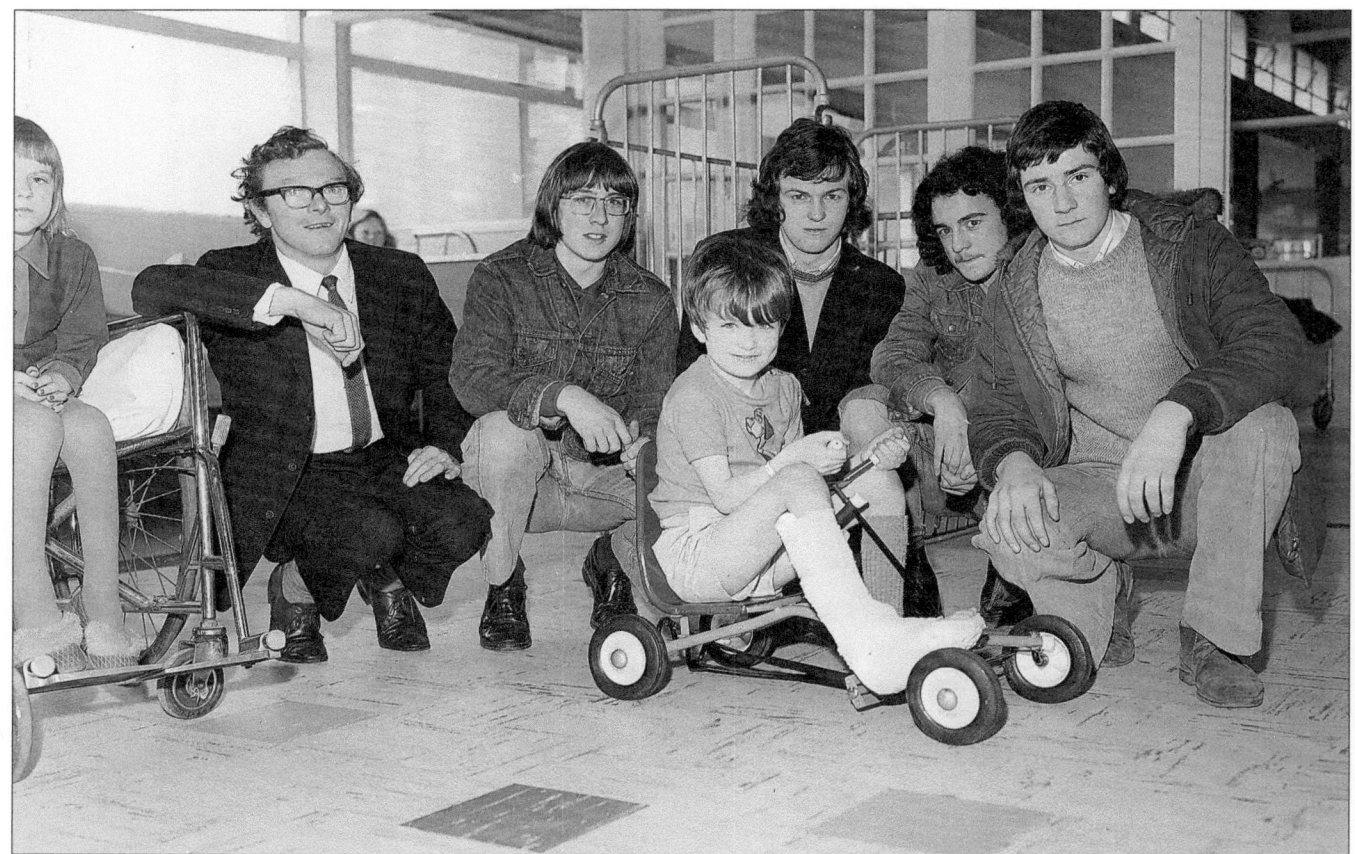

Bretby Orthopaedic Hospital has been closed but for most of this century it cared for children and adults with bone disorders from Burton, South Derbyshire and elsewhere. Getting better at Bretby could be fun, especially if you had the chance to ride a buggy like this.

A low bridge carrying the railway over Moor Street Bridge in Burton was for many years a danger to traffic, ripping the tops off tall vehicles including double decker coaches whose drivers were so unwise as to attempt to get under it. Eventually a warning system which involved flashing lights and wailing noises was installed to deter drivers whose vehicles would be unlikely to make it. The picture shows a vehicle which was damaged by the bridge in 1969. Luckily the driver was uninjured.

Another accident at Moor Street bridge. The route has now been closed to traffic and a nearby bridge carries the road over the railway.

When Alderman Harold Caulton became Mayor of Burton in 1969 he held his civic service at St Mark's Church, Winshill, the part of town where he lived and was a builder and funeral director. He appointed Winshill's vicar, the Rev W G Potts, as Mayor's Chaplain. A procession was led to the church by the Salvation Army Band and included councillors, police, St John Ambulance Brigade, Scouts, Cubs, Guides and Brownies. After local government reorganisation Mr Caulton became chairman of East Staffordshire Council and for some years that council's housing committee chairman.

Newhall Town Band led a parade of police, traders, miners, WRVS and other organisations to the civic service when Councillor A J Hough was elected chairman of Swadlincote Urban District Council in 1969. The Rev Jack Charlton, superintendent minister of South Derbyshire Methodist Circuit, conducted the service.

Way back in the 1930s barrel rolling races in Station Street were a popular local event. Brewery workers, who knew how to move empty kegs with a bobbing stick as part of their job, no easy task, proved that it could be fun. The idea was revived after the Second World War as part of the Whit Monday Cycling and Athletic Sports on a field at Stapenhill. Then in 1975 the races were reborn, this time as a Sunday event in High Street.

That first 1975 event was won by Marston's, represented by ex-Burton Albion player Chris Gilson and Colin Morris, who completed the three-quarter-mile course in 5.02 minutes. In the final they beat Barbarians, Police Cadet Philip Salisbury and welder Kevin Lovelock, whose time in the heats, 4.4 mins, was the fastest of the day. Delaney Gallay was third and Robirch fourth.

Two more pictures of the 1975 event. The old tradition was revived again in 1997, this time as the World Barrel Rolling Championships. Now entries come from eastern Europe and other distant lands.

Nostalgia for the days of steam will last at least as long as the old locos can be driven. Within a fortnight in 1975, *Mail* photographers lay in wait at Branston for three reminders of the good old days when we spoke of puffers or chuffers. The former Longmoor Military Railway 2-10-0 loco, Gordon, passed through on its way from Bridgnorth to Urlay Nook. A double headed train of old passenger stock on its way to the 150th anniversary of the Stockton-Darlington railway came through a few days later and then another loco bound for the same event was seen.

In these days when canal boating is a popular way of spending a holiday rather than of transporting coal, beer and other goods, Fradley Junction is a well known name. This hamlet near the village of Fradley is where boaters can switch from the Trent and Mersey Canal to the Coventry Canal or vice versa. Just as important, they can enjoy a pint or two in the Mucky Duck, officially known as the White Swan.

A glider lands at Burton's Boys' Grammar School. The power stations at Willington and Drakelow provided thermals which encouraged glider pilots to fly in the area. A thriving gliding club is based locally.

An attempt was made in the 1980s to restore the splendour of Burnaston House, a once spacious home that had fallen into decay. It was all in vain. The building was bulldozed to make way for the Toyota car factory in the 1990s.

The nearby Burnaston Aerodrome, once Derby's municipal airport, was later used for wartime pilot training, for a flying club and a small aero company. It, too, was swept away when Toyota came.

Tony Freeman, Swadlincote travel agent and former pop group member, made history by converting an unsightly slag heap, a relic of the South Derbyshire coal industry, into a ski slope. Nationwide, planners were so impressed with this magnificent example of land reclamation that they never again allowed permission for greenfield hill sites to be used for such slopes.

Tony, who ran the ski centre from the late 1980s to the mid-1990s. Now it is run by London-based John Nike.

The then managing director, Tony, with receptionist Miss Sue Brassington trying out the centre's toboggan run.

Not only did the ski slope offer great fun but...

...there was plenty of apres-ski atmosphere. Warming herself by the fire with instructors Nasco Hadjiski and Andy Siddal, both from Derby, is Lisa Smart.

Former gravel workings just off the A38 at Branston have become a favourite spot for recreation and nature study. These Canada geese share the water park with hundreds of human visitors.

For some years the water park was used by a sailing club and is still used for model boat racing and many other activities.

Dallow Lock, on the Trent and Mersey Canal at Burton.

Wychnor Lock, from which a short but pleasant walk on the towpath leads to…

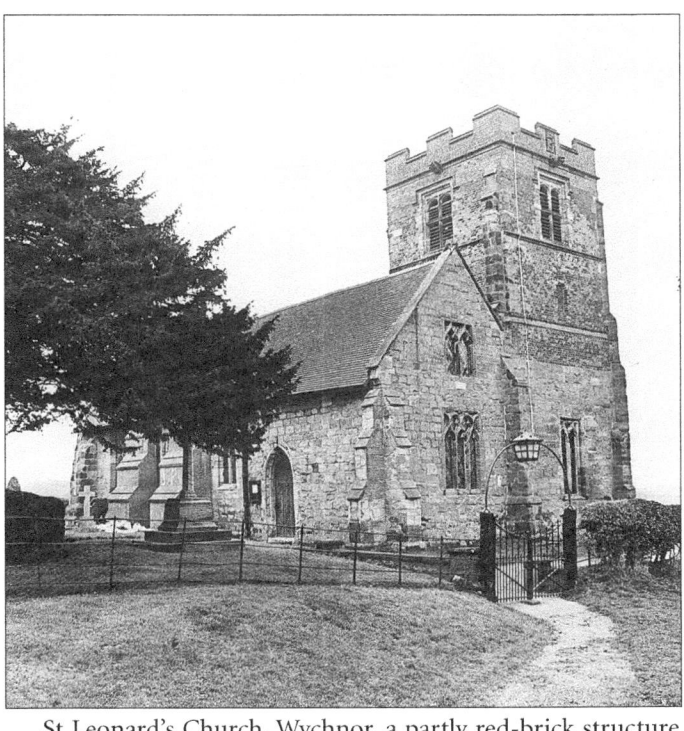

…St Leonard's Church, Wychnor, a partly red-brick structure serving a tiny community.

Bretby Pools in the grounds of Bretby Hall, which for many years served as an orthopaedic hospital, have been a Mecca for anglers. These two pictures show fishing in progress in a delightful setting.

These caves are another picturesque feature of the Bretby landscape.

Linton Heath lagoons.

Boats on the Dallow Lock on the Trent and Mersey Canal in Burton.

Floods on Burton Meadows near the Meadowside Leisure Centre.

Two pictures of the Dingle Bell which for some years took people on pleasure trips on the Trent from the Stapenhill end of the Ferry Bridge.

The coat of arms of Burton County Borough with its Latin motto, *Honor Alit Artes*, which is variously interpreted as Honour all the Arts, Honour Work, or even Honour Honour. This is part of the frontage of Burton Town Hall, now the headquarters of East Staffordshire Borough Council.

Another external feature of Burton Town Hall, an heraldic stone lion.

Michael Arthur Bass, first Baron Burton, presides over King Edward Place, named after a frequent guest at his Rangemore home. A popular local joke was that Lord Burton had his back to the church and his face towards the brewery. A little unfair. The church, St Paul's, was the gift of his father, Michael Thomas Bass, MP for Derby.

This 1910 picture shows a parade through Burton of the lifeboat given by the people of the town, which in long years of service saved many lives. In those days, as the picture shows, you could buy Burton-brewed Salt's beers in the Station Hotel, there were no short skirts and the men wore caps, bowlers, trilbies or straw hats.

On the left of this 1983 picture is the derelict Staffordshire Knot, once a popular Burton pub, now demolished. Before the junction with Union Street a modern block of shops and offices had already replaced the Station Street Methodist Church and its hall. On the right, the stone pillars near the bus shelter front the forecourt of Burton County Court.

Another example of the voluntary efforts, under the leadership of Burton Civic Society, to brighten Burton, in this case by bulb planting in Stapenhill Walk in 1984.

Plaques provided by Burton Civic Society draw attention to some of the town's more interesting buildings. The Queens Hotel, originally The Three Queens, was once a staging post for fast horse-drawn stage coaches like the Red Rover.

A much earlier view of Bridge Street looking towards Burton Bridge, or the Trent Bridge as it is better-known locally.

This picture in the archives of Burton Civic Society is the work of local photographer F. C. Buxton. It shows the former Nunneley's Brewery at Meadow Road, off Burton Bridge, in 1974. This building has now been converted into flats.

Demolition of a Bass building in High Street, Burton, in 1972. Though many old brewery buildings have gone, others have been preserved and enhanced as part of the town's industrial heritage.

The Dog and Partridge pub in New Street, Burton, being demolished in July, 1972, for redevelopment of the town centre. Its landlords had included Jack Stamps, the former Derby County star who was later player-manager of Burton Albion. The wheel turned full circle when Jack had a new Derby pub named after him.

In just one issue of the *Mail's* sister paper, the *Burton Observer and Chronicle* in 1973, there were pictures of three demolition jobs. These two pictures show the Coopers, a pub in Wetmore Road, following the traditional Burton craft of coopering into oblivion.

Another major demolition at that time was at the Shobnall Street premises of Yeomans, Cherry and Curtis, maltsters. The Worthington Maltings off The Hay came down at the same time.

The redevelopment of the central area of Burton in the late 1960s made use of derelict land and the sites of old buildings in the very heart of the town and the first major changes to the street scene for generations.

Curry's shop in Station Street, Burton, also had to go. The firm had premises in the central shopping precinct for some years afterwards and now has a much larger superstore at Wellington Road.

Drakelow Hall before 1932. Once it was the home of the Gresley family. A plan to turn it into a country club failed and later it was demolished. The power station was built on the site and grounds.

Dunstall Hall, home of Sir Bertram Hardy and later of Sir Robert Douglas. The Dunstall cricket ground, home of the Dunstall Cricket Fortnight in which teams from a wide area compete, is near the hall.

People and Places

Hundreds of people attended the 93rd annual Alrewas Agricultural Show on the Bycars Field. The Friesian classes were cancelled that year, 1972, but there were good entries for other cattle classes, horses, pigs, a gymkhana, with a record entry of 500 for the dog show. Attractions included sky divers. The show has long enjoyed a very high reputation in the Midlands although a comparatively small event of its kind.

A village horticultural show in Newhall.

Two pictures of the Meynell Hunt meeting at the New Inn, Needwood, near Burton, in 1973.

The Abbots Bromley Horn Dance, once a fertility rite, is performed each year. The 12-strong team, including a Robin Hood and a Maid Marion, carry ancient antlers on their shoulders and tour the farms and other settlements in and around the village. This 1972 picture was taken when they reached Blithfield Hall. Missing from the line-up that year was Douglas Fowell, whose family traditionally led the dance for many generations.

Stanton Village Hall fete in 1972.

It needed a farm elevator to help put in position the materials for the 5,000 cubic ft Guy Fawkes Night bonfire at Shobnall Fields in 1972. The fire was lit by the Mayor, Mrs Gertrude Pritchard, who also climbed a ladder to let off some of the fireworks.

About 15,000 people attended and a profit was made which Burton Police used to take children in care on a holiday. For several years a communal bonfire was organised by the police, then the fire service and others took over.

The Byerley Cup is one of the trophies open each year to local allotment holders and this picture was taken during judging in 1975. The popularity of growing your own may have slumped a little in recent years, and some allotment sites have disappeared in the name of progress, but there are still numbers of garden and allotment enthusiasts in Burton and district.

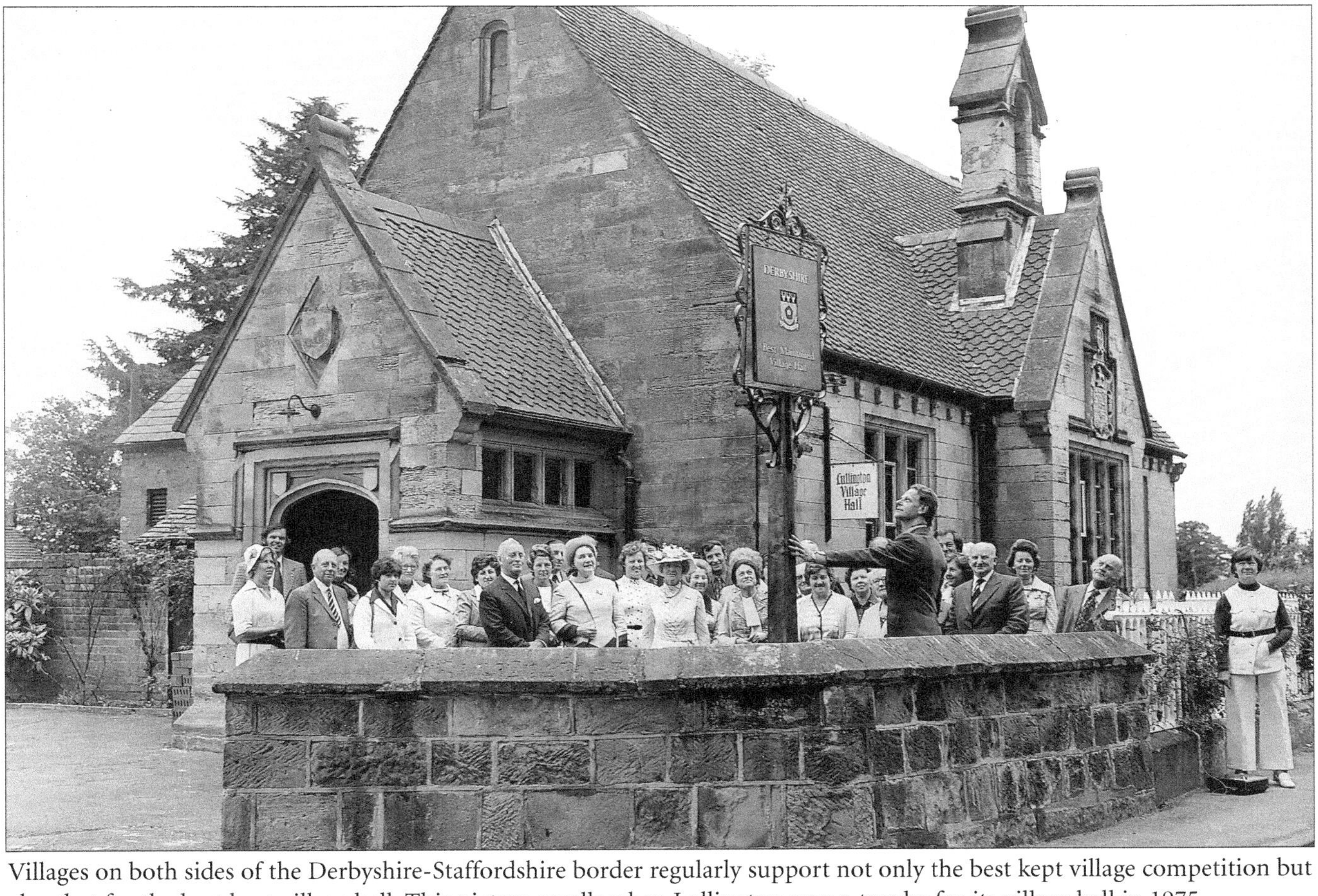

Villages on both sides of the Derbyshire-Staffordshire border regularly support not only the best kept village competition but also that for the best kept village hall. This picture recalls when Lullington won a trophy for its village hall in 1975.

Carnival organisers at Tutbury in 1975 were lucky in their choice of TV personality Gary Newbon as opener. He also compered the entire proceedings and judged the fancy dress. Burton Youth Band entertained and there was plenty to do and see.

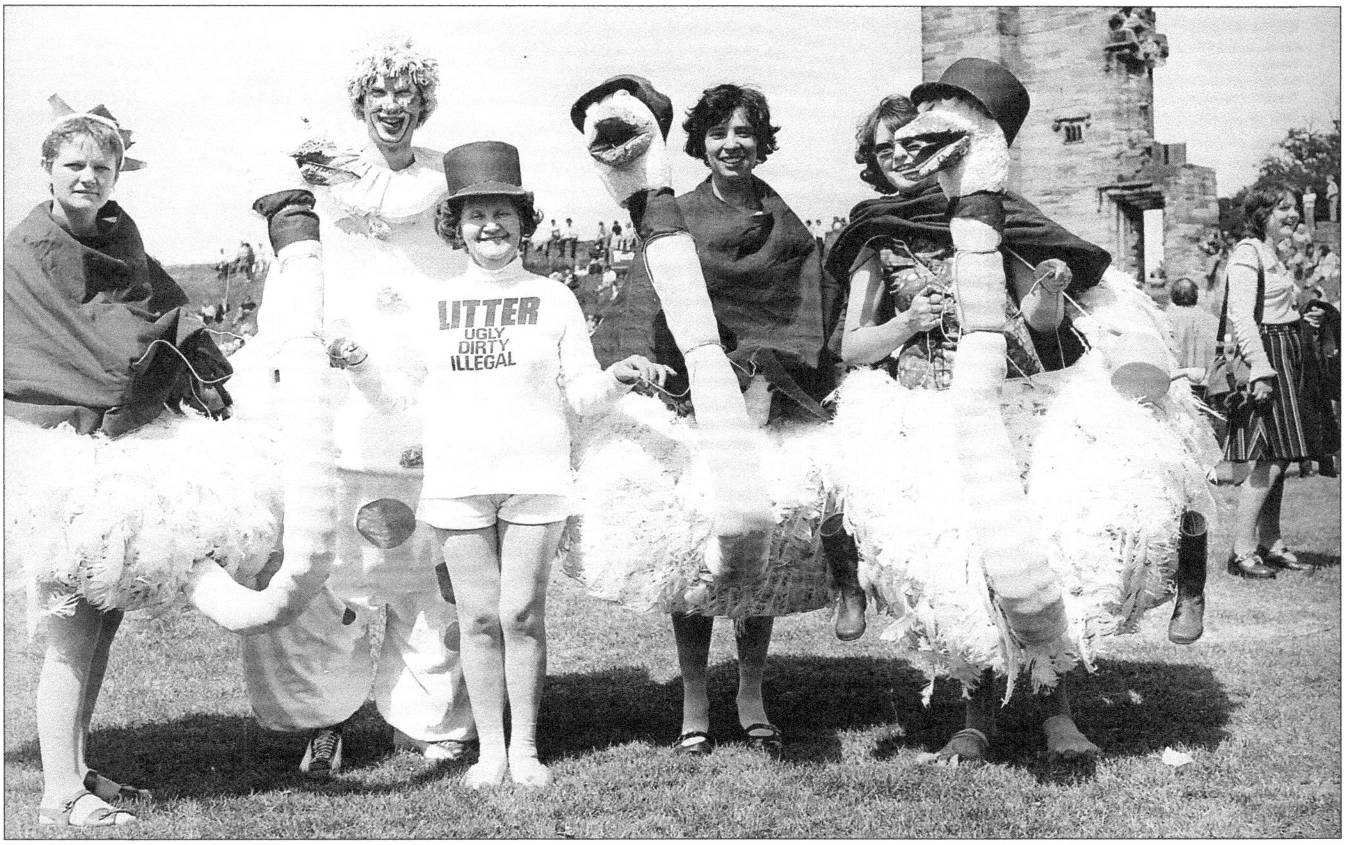
LITTER
UGLY
DIRTY
ILLEGAL

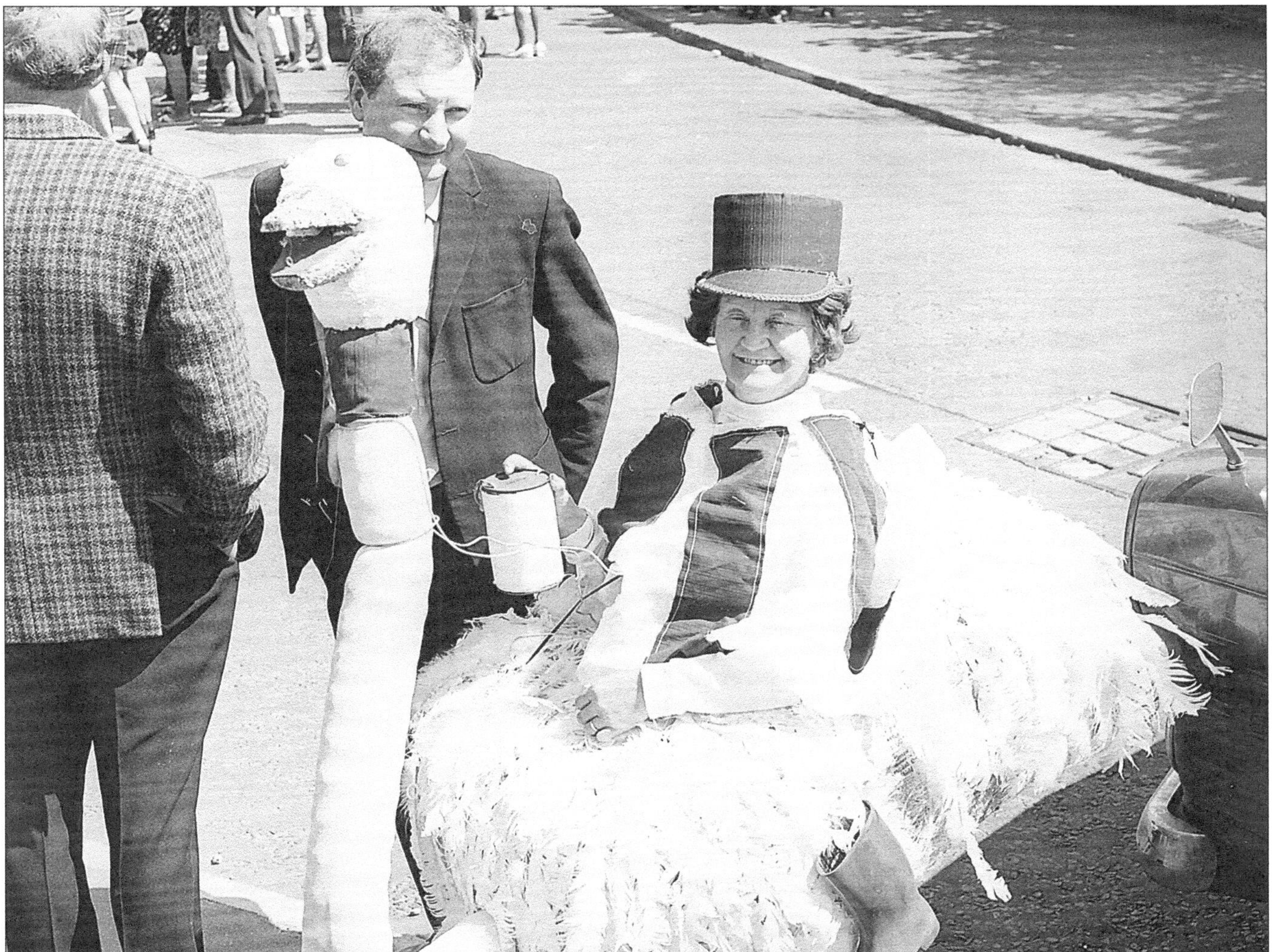

A church fete at Egginton, a Derbyshire village on the border with Staffordshire, separated from Stretton and Clay Mills by the River Dove.

Swadlincote Yellow Devils at Church Gresley.

Barton-under-Needwood Gala Day is a well-supported annual event.

There is always a wide range of attractions for children and adults at the gala.

Barton tug o'war team in action at the Barton fete on the Holland Sports Ground in 1972.

Spectators armed themselves with brollies under the threatening sky for the Shrove Tuesday pancake race in Barton-under-Needwood in 1973. Several local villages, and Burton itself, celebrate the day in this way.

Netherseal St Peter's Sports Club Gala Day. Netherseal, a tiny Derbyshire village, has always played an important part in the sporting life of the area. Its tennis club has a particularly good reputation and the great Fred Perry once visited and played there.

Quizzes are very popular in the area, and since townsfolk and country folk live so near each other it is not surprising that sometimes the questions are about the countryside. That was the theme of this South Derbyshire quiz contest 30 years ago.

The local Cooperative Society Queen at Burton's St Paul's Institute in 1973.

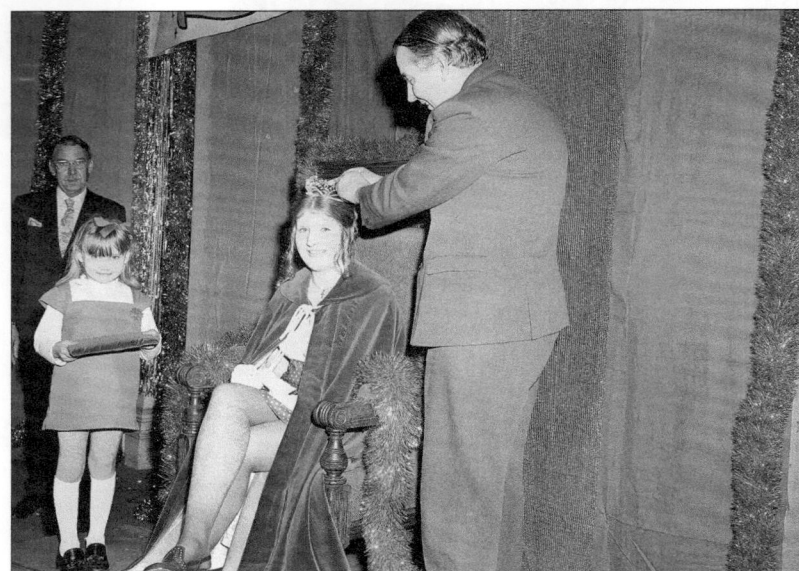

Burton Municipal Band give a concert at Hilton House.

A special occasion for Walton-on-Trent Women's Institute, which held a jubilee dinner in 1972.

The May Ball of the National Society for the Prevention of Cruelty to Children at Rangemore Hall in 1969.

Part of the audience for…

…a performance by Burton Police Minstrels at Bend Oak House old people's home in Winshill. The minstrels were a valued part of the entertainment scene in Burton and district for many years, before anyone thought there was anything politically incorrect about blacking up.

A view of part of the audience for a concert at Pingle School in Swadlincote in 1973…

…and the band they were listening to.

Swadlincote Salvation Army Silver Lining Club celebrating its first anniversary in 1969.

High Street, Swadlincote, showing the Nag's Head, a popular rendezvous for drinks and meals for many years.

Swadlincote Darby and Joan Club Choir has long had a good reputation locally. This picture was taken in 1973.

The Gresley Arms at Castle Gresley, from an old glass negative in the *Burton Mail* archives.

The Nag's Head in Swadlincote where for many years the much respected landlady was Mrs Warren, known as Auntie Min.

At Winshill, as in many other churchyards, the gravestones have been moved to enable the area to be mown and kept tidy. This picture shows the operation in progress in 1975.

Restoration of the bell tower of Chilcote Church near Netherseal in 1972.

The non-conformist churches have always been strong in South Derbyshire.

We've all heard Lord Northcliffe's dictum: dog bites man, that's not news; man bites dog, that's news. An odd variation on the theme had a *Mail* photographer heading for Sudbury in 1972 for a picture of an Alsatian bitten by a pike.

This picture in *Burton Mail* archives was mysteriously and prophetically labelled Group Spice. It was taken some 20 years before we heard of the chart-topping Spice Girls.

Linton Village Hall was opened in 1972, just 26 years after it was first thought of. Villagers raised £13,000 to make it possible. The opener was Councillor W L Bates, who represented Linton on Repton Rural District Council.

The Gurkhas marching through High Street, Burton, in 1975.

Joe Fearn, local band leader and piano entertainer, one time swimming and diving champion, keen motorcyclist and a businessman who has kept a pub, run a filling station, helped run a music shop and much else. He found time in 1972 to pose for this picture when taking delivery of his Ford Volkswagen from Graham Fearn, sales manager of Fenn's garage in Derby Road. The first car to be registered in Burton, FA 1, was a 10hp Wolseley owned by Mr George Frederick Reading. That was in December, 1903.

Burton branch of the Women's Royal Voluntary Services celebrated its move into new headquarters in Union Street by holding an open day in 1972. These were some of the people who were active in the movement at that time: (left to right, back) Mrs L Griffiths, emergency welfare organiser, Mrs R. B. Barratt, her deputy, Mrs F. E. Dring, general services organiser, front, Miss D. M. Fraser, superintendent nursing officer for public health, Mrs M. M. Dean, meals organiser, Mrs D. M. Wright, MBE, county borough organiser, Mrs W. G. Walton MBE. How rapidly things change: that headquarters building was demolished in the late 1990s to make way for a Sainsbury's supermarket.

A British Red Cross Society inspection at Granville School, Woodville, in 1975.

A flower festival at Gresley Parish Church.

Children skating on the River Trent at Burton, near the Andressey Bridge.